Preface:

Greetings, intrepid traveler of the digital landscapes!

In your hands rests not just a book, but a key to the boundless world of web development—welcome to "HTMLicious CSSentials & JavaScriptopia: Mastering the Web Development Symphony." This isn't a mere guide; it's an invitation to embark on an extraordinary journey, unraveling the intricacies of HTML, CSS, and JavaScript.

A Unique Learning Odyssey:

Prepare to embark on a learning odyssey where each chapter isn't just a waypoint; it's a portal to undiscovered territories. As you traverse the landscapes of HTMLicious, sail the seas of CSSentials, and ascend the peaks of JavaScriptopia, embrace the uniqueness of your learning expedition. Here, knowledge isn't static; it's a living, breathing entity waiting to be explored.

Venturing into the Unknown:

Beyond these pages, a vast horizon of knowledge beckons. The Mozilla Developer Network (MDN) isn't just a reference; it's a treasure trove. Let each chapter be a compass, guiding you to delve deeper into the documentation, charting your course through the ever-evolving digital wilderness.

The Crucible of Practice:

Learning flourishes in the crucible of practice. Pause, experiment, and code alongside the concepts presented. Challenge yourself to not just understand but to create, break, and mend. In the crucible, skills are honed, and mastery emerges.

Read, Reflect, Resonate:

This isn't a sprint; it's a transformative journey. Read with intention, reflect on the "why" beneath the code, and let the concepts resonate with your unique understanding. Each chapter isn't just information; it's a musical note in the symphony of your learning. Understand its melody, and you' ll wield the power to compose your web creations with finesse.

An Overture to Creativity:

Consider this not just a handbook but an overture to creativity—an invitation to explore, experiment, and evolve. With each flip of the page, remember: you're not just a reader; you're a creator, a composer, and a developer.

Embark on the Odyssey:

So, intrepid explorer, let the odyssey commence! Dive into the rich tapestry of HTMLicious, traverse the scenic landscapes of CSSentials, and ascend the heights of JavaScriptopia. The web awaits, ready for your unique touch.

Beyond Mastery: The Next Symphony:

As you conclude this handbook, envision it as the prologue to your web development saga. Venture further by exploring JavaScript frameworks like React—an expansive realm awaiting your mastery. Let this book be a springboard for small projects, for in them lies the true crucible of learning. Whether it's crafting a personal website, developing a portfolio, or creating a dynamic web app, projects are your proving grounds.

A New Chapter Awaits:

With this book as your compass and MDN as your map, the journey doesn't end here; it evolves. Embrace the ever-changing landscape of web development, seek new challenges, and let curiosity be your guide. This isn't just a prelude; it's an opening chord to a symphony of possibilities.

Happy and adventurous exploring!

The Author

1. Introduction to Web Development

Welcome to the exciting world of web development! This introductory section provides a glimpse into the fundamental concepts that shape the web.

1.1 Understanding the Web Development Stack

Frontend (Client-Side): Dive into the elements that users interact with directly. Explore HTML for structure, CSS for styling, and JavaScript for interactivity.
Backend (Server-Side): Uncover the server-side technologies responsible for processing requests and managing data.
Database: Learn about databases and their role in storing and retrieving information.

1.2 Importance of HTML, CSS, and JavaScript

HTML Basics: Grasp the foundation of web content structure, from documents to headings and paragraphs.
CSS Basics: Delve into styling elements using selectors, properties, and the box model.
JavaScript Basics: Uncover the scripting language's power for creating dynamic and interactive web pages.

1.3 How the Web Works and Core Concepts

1.3.1 Client-Server Model

In web development, the client-server model is fundamental. Clients (browsers) send requests to servers, which respond with data.

```html
<!-- index.html (Client-Side) -->
<!DOCTYPE html><html lang="en">
<head>
 <title>Client-Side Example</title>
</head>
<body>
 <h1>Welcome to the Client-Side</h1>
 <p>This content is delivered to the user's browser.</p>
</body></html>
```

1.3.2 HTTP/HTTPS Protocols

HTTP (Hypertext Transfer Protocol) and HTTPS (Hypertext Transfer Protocol Secure) are protocols governing data transfer.

```html
<!-- protocol.html -->
<!DOCTYPE html>
<html lang="en">
<head>
  <meta charset="UTF-8">
  <meta name="viewport" content="width=device-width, initial-scale=1.0">
  <title>HTTP/HTTPS Example</title>
</head>
<body>
  <h1>Understanding HTTP/HTTPS</h1>
  <p>Your data is transmitted using HTTP or its secure version,
HTTPS.</p>
</body></html>
```

1.3.3 DNS and Hosting

Domain Name System (DNS) translates domain names to IP addresses. Hosting services store and serve web content.

```html
<!-- dns_hosting.html -->
<!DOCTYPE html>
<html lang="en">
<head>
  <meta charset="UTF-8">
  <meta name="viewport" content="width=device-width, initial-scale=1.0">
  <title>DNS and Hosting</title>
</head>
<body>
  <h1>Decoding DNS and Hosting</h1>
  <p>Your domain, like www.example.com, is translated to an IP address by
DNS for hosting.</p>
</body></html>
```

1.3.4 Web Browsers

Browsers render and interpret web content. They play a crucial role in user interaction with websites.

Sample HTML code ☐

```html
<!-- browsers.html -->
<!DOCTYPE html>
<html lang="en">
<head>
 <meta charset="UTF-8">
 <meta name="viewport" content="width=device-width, initial-scale=1.0">
 <title>Web Browsers</title>
</head>
<body>
 <h1>Exploring Web Browsers</h1>
 <p>Browsers like Chrome, Firefox, and Safari interpret HTML, CSS, and
JavaScript to display websites.</p>
</body>
</html>
```

1.4 Create Your First HTML Page Using Visual Studio Code

Step 1: Install Visual Studio Code

If you haven't already installed Visual Studio Code, you can download and install it from the official website: Visual Studio Code

Step 2: Open Visual Studio Code

Once installed, open Visual Studio Code.

Step 3: Create a New HTML File

Click on "File" in the top-left corner.
Select "New File" to create a new file.
Save the file with an HTML extension (e.g., index.html). Use the .html extension to indicate that it's an HTML file.

Step 4: Set Up the HTML Structure

In your index.html file, set up the basic HTML structure:

```html
<!DOCTYPE html>
<html lang="en">
<head>
 <meta charset="UTF-8">
 <meta name="viewport" content="width=device-width, initial-scale=1.0">
 <title>Your First HTML Page</title>
</head>
<body>
 <h1>Hello, World!</h1>
</body>
</html>
```

This HTML structure includes the document type declaration, HTML root element, head section with meta tags, and a simple "Hello, World!" message in the body.

Step 5: Save the File

Save the changes to your index.html file.

Step 6: Open in Browser

Right-click on the index.html file in Visual Studio Code.
Select "Open with Live Server" if you have the Live Server extension installed. This will open your HTML file in a browser with live reloading.
Or
Right-click on the index.html file.
Select "Copy Path."
Open your preferred browser.
Paste the path into the browser's address bar and press Enter.
You should now see your "Hello, World!" message displayed in the browser.

Step 7: Use It for Other Tutorials

Now that you've created your first HTML page, you can use it as a starting point for other tutorials. Simply open the index.html file in Visual Studio Code, make modifications or add new elements as instructed in other tutorials, and see the changes live in your browser.

Congratulations! You've successfully created and viewed your first HTML page using Visual Studio Code. Feel free to build on this foundation as you explore more tutorials and concepts in web development.

2. HTML Basics

2.1 Understanding the Structure of an HTML Document

2.1.1 Document Structure Overview

HTML documents have a predefined structure that includes a declaration, an opening HTML tag, and divisions into head and body sections.

2.1.2 HTML Document Skeleton

Here's a basic example of an HTML document structure:

```html
<!DOCTYPE html>
<html>
 <head>
 <!-- Metadata and links to external resources go here -->
 </head>
 <body>
 <!-- Content visible to users goes here -->
 </body>
</html>
```

2.1.2.1 Head and Body Sections

The <head> section contains metadata, and the <body> section contains the visible content. Each section is essential for proper HTML structure.

2.1.3 Head and Body Sections

Further exploration of the <head> and <body> sections and their specific roles in an HTML document.

2.2 HTML Tags and Elements

2.2.1 Inline vs. Block-Level Elements

HTML elements are categorized as inline or block-level. Inline elements don't start on a new line and only take up as much width as necessary, while block-level elements start on a new line and take up the full width available. For example:

```html
<span>This is an inline element</span>
<div>This is a block-level element</div>
```

2.2.2 Semantic HTML5 Elements

Semantic elements provide meaning to the structure. Here are examples:

2.2.2.1 <article>, <section>, <nav>

```html
<article>
 <h2>Article Title</h2>
 <p>Article content goes here.</p>
</article>

<section>
 <h2>Section Title</h2>
 <p>Section content goes here.</p>
</section>

<nav>
 <ul>
 <li><a href="#">Home</a></li>
 <li><a href="#">About</a></li>
 </ul>
</nav>
```

2.2.2.2 <header>, <footer>, <main>

```html
<header>
 <h1>Website Header</h1>
</header>

<main>
 <h2>Main Content</h2>
 <p>Main content goes here.</p>
</main>

<footer>
 <p>&copy; 2023 My Website</p>
</footer>
```

2.2.3 HTML Attributes

2.2.3.1 Understanding HTML Attributes

Attributes provide additional information about HTML elements. For example:

```html
<img src="image.jpg" alt="Description">
```

2.2.3.2 Global Attributes

Attributes like class and id are global and can be applied to various elements. They play a key role in styling and scripting.

```html
<div class="container" id="main-container">Content goes here</div>
```

2.2.3.3 Common Attributes for Specific Tags

Certain tags have attributes specific to them. For instance, the <a> tag has an href attribute for specifying the hyperlink.

html
Copy code
```
<a href="https://example.com">Visit Example</a>
```

2.3 Essential HTML Tags

2.3.1 Headings and Paragraphs

2.3.1.1 Heading Levels (h1 to h6)

Headings range from <h1> (highest importance) to <h6> (lowest importance). They provide structure to your content.

```
<h1>Main Heading</h1>
<h2>Subheading</h2>
```

2.3.1.2 <p> Tag and Text Formatting

The <p> tag is used for paragraphs, and text formatting can be achieved with tags like <strong> for bold and <em> for emphasis.

```
<p>This is a paragraph with <strong>strong</strong> and
<em>emphasized</em> text.</p>
```

2.3.2 Lists (Ordered and Unordered)

2.3.2.1 Creating Ordered Lists (<ol>)

```
<ol>
 <li>First item</li>
 <li>Second item</li>
</ol>
```

2.3.2.2 Unordered Lists (<ul>) and List Items (<li>)

```
<ul>
```

```
    <li>Item 1</li>
    <li>Item 2</li>
</ul>
```

2.3.2.3 Customizing List Styles

Apply CSS to customize list styles. For example:

```
ul {
    list-style-type: square;
}
```

2.3.3 Links and Anchors

2.3.3.1 Creating Hyperlinks with <a>

Create hyperlinks with the <a> tag. Specify the target URL using the href attribute.

```
<a href="https://example.com">Visit Example</a>
```

2.3.3.2 Linking to External Resources

Link to external resources by providing the full URL in the href attribute.

```
<a href="https://external-resource.com">External Resource</a>
```

2.3.3.3 Anchor Tags and Internal Page Links

Internal links within the same page are created using anchor tags (<a>) with appropriate href values.

```
<a href="#section">Jump to Section</a>
```

```
<section id="section">
 <!-- Section content goes here -->
</section>
```

2.3.4 Images and Multimedia

2.3.4.1 Embedding Images with <img>

Embedding images is done with the <img> tag. Include the src attribute with the image URL.

```
<img src="image.jpg" alt="Description">
```

2.3.4.2 Image Attributes (alt, width, height)

Specify attributes like alt for alternative text and width/height for image dimensions.

```
<img src="image.jpg" alt="Description" width="300" height="200">
```

2.3.4.3 Including Audio and Video (<audio>, <video>)

Use the <audio> and <video> tags for embedding audio and video content. Set the src attribute to the media file.

```
<audio controls>
 <source src="audio.mp3" type="audio/mp3">
 Your browser does not support the audio tag.
</audio>
```

continue...

```
<video controls width="400" height="300">
 <source src="video.mp4" type="video/mp4">
 Your browser does not support the video tag.
</video>
```

2.4 HTML Forms

2.4.1 Creating Forms and Form Elements

2.4.1.1 Form Structure and <form> Tag

Create forms with the <form> tag. Include input elements like text fields and buttons within the form.

```
<form action="/submit" method="post">
 <label for="username">Username:</label>
 <input type="text" id="username" name="username">

 <input type="submit" value="Submit">
</form>
```

2.4.1.2 Input Elements (text, password, radio, checkbox)

Input elements include text fields (<input type="text">), password fields (<input type="password">), radio buttons, and checkboxes.

```
<input type="text" placeholder="Enter text">
<input type="password" placeholder="Enter password">
<input type="radio" name="gender" value="male"> Male</input>
<input type="checkbox" name="subscribe" checked> Subscribe</input>
```

2.4.1.3 Select Boxes and Textareas

Select boxes (<select>) create dropdown menus, and textareas (<textarea>) allow multiline text input.

```
<select>
 <option value="option1">Option 1</option>
 <option value="option2">Option 2</option>
```

```
</select>

<textarea rows="4" cols="50">Enter text here...</textarea>
```

2.4.2 Form Validation with JavaScript

2.4.2.1 Client-Side Form Validation

Use JavaScript for client-side form validation. Check input values before submitting the form.

```
<script>
function validateForm() {
var x = document.forms["myForm"]["fname"].value;
if (x == "") {
alert("Name must be filled out");
return false;
}
}
</script>

<form name="myForm" onsubmit="return validateForm()" method="post">
 Name: <input type="text" name="fname">
 <input type="submit" value="Submit">
</form>
```

2.4.2.2 HTML5 Form Validation Attributes

HTML5 introduces attributes like required and pattern for built-in form validation.

```html
<input type="text" name="username" required>
<input type="text" pattern="[0-9]{3}" title="Three digit number">
```

2.4.2.3 Custom JavaScript Validation Functions

Write custom JavaScript functions to handle specific form validation requirements.

```html
<script>
 function validateEmail() {
 var email = document.getElementById("email").value;
 var regex = /^\S+@\S+\.\S+$/;
 if (!regex.test(email)) {
 alert("Invalid email format");
 return false;
 }
 }
</script>
<form onsubmit="return validateEmail()">
 Email: <input type="text" id="email">
 <input type="submit" value="Submit">
</form>
```

2.4.3 Styling Forms with CSS

2.4.3.1 Styling Input Elements

Apply CSS styles to input elements for a more visually appealing form.

```css
input[type="text"] {
    width: 200px;
    padding: 5px;
    margin: 5px;
 }
```

2.4.3.2 Customizing Form Layouts

Use CSS to customize the layout of the entire form, adjusting spacing and alignment.

```css
form {
    width: 50%;
    margin: 0 auto;
}
```

2.4.3.3 Handling Form States (focus, hover, active)

Apply styles for different form states (e.g., focus, hover, active) to enhance user interaction.

```css
input[type="text"]:hover {
    background-color: #f0f0f0;
}
```

2.5 HTML Tables

2.5.1 Creating Basic Tables

Tables are created using the <table> tag, rows with <tr>, and data cells with <td>.

```html
<table>
<tr>
<td>Row 1, Cell 1</td>
<td>Row 1, Cell 2</td>
</tr>
<tr>
<td>Row 2, Cell 1</td>
<td>Row 2, Cell 2</td>
</tr>
</table>
```

2.5.2 Advanced Table Features

Explore advanced table features like colspan and rowspan to merge cells and create more complex layouts.

```html
<table>
<tr><td colspan="2">Merged Cells</td></tr>
<tr>
<td rowspan="2">Row 2, Cell 1</td>
<td>Row 2, Cell 2</td>
</tr>
</table>
```

2.5.3 Styling Tables with CSS

Enhance the visual presentation of tables using CSS. Apply styles to the table, rows, and cells for a polished look.

```css
table {
    border-collapse: collapse;
    width: 100%;
}

td, th {
    border: 1px solid #ddd;
    padding: 8px;
    text-align: left;
}

th {
    background-color: #f2f2f2;
}
```

These examples provide a hands-on introduction to HTML concepts, offering a foundation for building web pages and forms. You can use these as starting points for more complex projects and explore additional HTML and CSS features as you progress in web development.

3. HTML Canvas

3.1 Introduction to HTML Canvas

3.1.1 Creating a Canvas Element

HTML canvas provides a powerful platform for dynamic graphics and visualizations on the web. To start, you'll need to create a canvas element within your HTML:

```html
<!DOCTYPE html>
<html lang="en">
<head>
 <meta charset="UTF-8">
 <meta name="viewport" content="width=device-width, initial-scale=1.0">
 <title>Canvas Introduction</title>
</head>
<body>
 <canvas id="myCanvas" width="400" height="200"></canvas>
 <!-- Additional content or scripts can follow -->
</body>
</html>
```

3.1.2 Setting Canvas Dimensions

Adjusting the canvas dimensions is essential for tailoring it to your specific design. This can be achieved in the HTML or dynamically using JavaScript:

```html
<canvas id="myCanvas" width="800" height="400"></canvas>
```

3.1.3 Drawing Basic Shapes (Rectangles, Circles, Lines)

Now, let's delve into drawing basic shapes on the canvas. Using JavaScript, you can create rectangles, circles, and lines with ease:

```
<script>
  var canvas = document.getElementById("myCanvas");
  var ctx = canvas.getContext("2d");

  // Drawing a rectangle
  ctx.fillStyle = "#FF0000";
  ctx.fillRect(20, 20, 100, 50);

  // Drawing a circle
  ctx.beginPath();
  ctx.arc(200, 50, 30, 0, 2 * Math.PI);
  ctx.fillStyle = "#00FF00";
  ctx.fill();

  // Drawing a line
  ctx.moveTo(250, 20);
  ctx.lineTo(350, 70);
  ctx.strokeStyle = "#0000FF";
  ctx.stroke();
</script>
```

3.2 Working with Paths and Text

3.2.1 Defining Paths and Strokes

Paths are a fundamental concept in canvas drawing. They allow you to create complex shapes and define strokes for enhanced visual appeal:

```html
<script>
  var canvas = document.getElementById("myCanvas");
  var ctx = canvas.getContext("2d");

  // Creating a path
  ctx.beginPath();
  ctx.moveTo(20, 100);
  ctx.lineTo(100, 100);
  ctx.lineTo(60, 150);
  ctx.closePath();

  // Applying a stroke
  ctx.lineWidth = 2;
  ctx.strokeStyle = "#FF00FF";
  ctx.stroke();
</script>
```

3.2.2 Adding Text to the Canvas

Incorporating text into your canvas adds informative and engaging elements. Customize the font, size, and color to match your design:

```html
<script>
  var canvas = document.getElementById("myCanvas");
  var ctx = canvas.getContext("2d");

  // Adding text
  ctx.font = "20px Arial";
  ctx.fillStyle = "#000000";
  ctx.fillText("Hello, Canvas!", 20, 180);
</script>
```

3.2.3 Styling and Formatting Text

Styling text goes beyond mere content. You can experiment with different fonts, sizes, and styles to achieve the desired visual effect:

```
<script>
 var canvas = document.getElementById("myCanvas");
 var ctx = canvas.getContext("2d");

 // Styling text
 ctx.font = "italic bold 24px Times New Roman";
 ctx.fillStyle = "#3366FF";
 ctx.fillText("Styled Text", 20, 180);
</script>
```

3.3 Handling User Interaction

3.3.1 Capturing Mouse Events

Canvas interaction becomes dynamic when combined with user input. Capture mouse events to create responsive and interactive canvases:

```
<script>
 var canvas = document.getElementById("myCanvas");
 var ctx = canvas.getContext("2d");

 canvas.addEventListener("mousemove", function(event) {
 var x = event.clientX - canvas.getBoundingClientRect().left;
 var y = event.clientY - canvas.getBoundingClientRect().top;

 // Respond to mouse movement
 ctx.clearRect(0, 0, canvas.width, canvas.height);
 ctx.fillText("Mouse Position: " + x + ", " + y, 20, 180);
 });
</script>
```

3.3.2 Responding to Keyboard Input

Extend canvas interactivity by responding to keyboard input. Here's a simple example that moves a drawn object using arrow keys:

```
<script>
var canvas = document.getElementById("myCanvas");
var ctx = canvas.getContext("2d");
var x = 50;
var y = 50;

window.addEventListener("keydown", function(event) {
// Respond to arrow key presses
switch (event.key) {
case "ArrowUp":
y -= 5;
break;
case "ArrowDown":
y += 5;
break;
case "ArrowLeft":
x -= 5;
break;
case "ArrowRight":
x += 5;
break;
}

// Redraw the object
ctx.clearRect(0, 0, canvas.width, canvas.height);
ctx.fillRect(x, y, 30, 30);
});
</script>
```

3.3.3 Creating Interactive Canvas Elements

Combine mouse and keyboard events to create fully interactive canvas elements. Here's a sample of a clickable button:

```
<script>
var canvas = document.getElementById("myCanvas");
var ctx = canvas.getContext("2d");


var button = {
x: 50,
y: 100,
width: 100,
height: 40
};


canvas.addEventListener("click", function(event) {
var mouseX = event.clientX - canvas.getBoundingClientRect().left;
var mouseY = event.clientY - canvas.getBoundingClientRect().top;

// Check if the click is within the button area
if (mouseX > button.x && mouseX < button.x + button.width &&
mouseY > button.y && mouseY < button.y + button.height) {
alert("Button Clicked!");
}
});


// Draw the button
ctx.fillStyle = "#008080";
ctx.fillRect(button.x, button.y, button.width, button.height);
ctx.fillStyle = "#FFFFFF";
ctx.font = "bold 16px Arial";
ctx.fillText("Click Me", button.x + 15, button.y + 25);
</script>
```

3.4 Animations with Canvas

3.4.1 Frame-by-Frame Animation

Create captivating animations on the canvas by leveraging frame-by-frame rendering. Here's a basic example of moving a shape across the canvas:

```html
<!DOCTYPE html>
<html lang="en">
<head>
    <title>Canvas Animation</title>
    <style>
        canvas {
            border: 1px solid #000;
        }
    </style>
</head>
<body>
    <!-- Create a canvas element with an id -->
    <canvas id="myCanvas" width="600" height="200"></canvas>
    <script>
        // Get the canvas element and its 2d context
        var canvas = document.getElementById("myCanvas");
        var ctx = canvas.getContext("2d");
        // Initial x-coordinate for the rectangle
        var x = 0;
        // Animation function
        function animate() {
            // Clear the canvas
            ctx.clearRect(0, 0, canvas.width, canvas.height);
            // Draw a moving rectangle
            ctx.fillRect(x, 50, 30, 30);
            // Update the position for the next frame
            x += 2;
            requestAnimationFrame(animate);
        }
        // Start the animation loop
        animate();
    </script>
</body>
</html>
```

4. CSS Basics

4.1 Selectors and Properties

4.1.1 Understanding CSS Selectors

CSS selectors are essential for targeting HTML elements and applying styles. Let's explore various selector types:

4.1.1.1 Type Selectors

Type selectors target specific HTML elements. For example, to style all paragraphs:

```css
p {
    color: blue;
}
```

4.1.1.2 Class Selectors

Class selectors target elements with a specific class attribute. Apply styles to elements with the "highlight" class:

```css
.highlight {
    background-color: yellow;
}
```

4.1.1.3 ID Selectors

ID selectors target a unique element with a specific ID attribute. Style an element with the "header" ID:

```css
#header {
    font-size: 24px;
}
```

4.1.1.4 Attribute Selectors

Attribute selectors let you target elements based on their attributes. For example, select all input elements with a type of "text":

```css
input[type="text"] {
    border: 1px solid #ccc;
}
```

4.1.1.5 Pseudo-classes and Pseudo-elements

Pseudo-classes and pseudo-elements provide ways to select elements based on their state or position. Style the hovered link:

```css
a:hover {
    text-decoration: underline;
}
```

4.1.2 Common CSS Properties

4.1.2.1 Text Properties (font, color, size)

Customize text appearance using properties like font, color, and size:

```css
body {
    font-family: 'Arial', sans-serif;
    color: #333;
    font-size: 16px;
}
```

4.1.2.2 Box Properties (width, height, margin, padding)

Control the size and spacing of elements with box properties:

```css
.box {
    width: 200px;
    height: 150px;
    margin: 20px;
    padding: 10px;
}
```

4.1.2.3 Display Property

The display property influences the type of box an element generates. For example, make a list display horizontally:

```css
ul {
    display: flex;
    justify-content: space-around;
}
```

4.1.2.4 Positioning (static, relative, absolute, fixed)

Positioning properties determine the layout of elements. Position a div relative to its normal position:

```css
.relative-box {
    position: relative;
    top: 20px;
    left: 30px;
}
```

4.2 Colors, Backgrounds, and Borders

4.2.1 Applying Colors to Elements

4.2.1.1 Hexadecimal, RGB, and HSL Color Notations
Specify colors using various notations:

```css
#hex-color {
    color: #ff0000;
}


.rgb-color {
  background-color: rgb(255, 0, 0);
}


.hsl-color {
  border: 2px solid hsl(0, 100%, 50%);
}
```

4.2.1.2 Named Colors
Use named colors for simplicity:

```css
.named-color {
    color: red;
}
```

4.2.1.3 Opacity and RGBA
Adjust element opacity using RGBA:

```css
.transparent-box {
    background-color: rgba(0, 128, 255, 0.5);
}
```

4.2.2 Working with Backgrounds

4.2.2.1 Background Color
Apply background color to elements:

```css
.background-color {
    background-color: #f2f2f2;
}
```

4.2.2.2 Background Images
Add background images to elements:

```css
.background-image {
    background-image: url('image.jpg');
    background-size: cover;
}
```

4.2.2.3 Background Repeat and Positioning
Control background repetition and positioning:

```css
.repeated-background {
    background-image: url('pattern.png');
    background-repeat: repeat-x;
    background-position: center top;
}
```

4.2.3 Styling Borders and Outlines

4.2.3.1 Border Styles (solid, dashed, dotted)

Define border styles for elements:

```css
.border-style {
    border: 2px solid #333;
}

.dashed-border {
    border: 1px dashed #999;
}
```

4.2.3.2 Border Width and Color

Adjust border width and color:

```css
.thick-border {
    border-width: 4px;
}

.colored-border {
    border: 2px solid red;
}
```

4.2.3.3 Outline Property

Use the outline property for non-rectangular borders:

```css
.outlined-box {
    outline: 2px solid green;
}
```

4.3 Margin, Padding, and Box Model

4.3.1 Understanding Margin and Padding

4.3.1.1 Margin Collapse

Be aware of margin collapse, especially in vertical margins between adjacent elements:

```css
.collapsible-margin {
    margin-bottom: 20px;
}


.non-collapsible-margin {
    margin-top: 30px;
}
```

4.3.2 Box Model Essentials

4.3.2.1 Content, Padding, Border, Margin

The box model comprises content, padding, border, and margin. Adjust each for precise control:

```css
.box-model-example {
    width: 200px;
    padding: 20px;
    border: 2px solid #333;
    margin: 10px;
}
```

4.3.2.2 Box Sizing Property

Alter box sizing for improved layout calculations:

```css
.sized-box {
    box-sizing: border-box;
    width: 200px;
    padding: 20px;
    border: 2px solid #333;
}
```

4.3.2.3 Calculating Total Element Width and Height

Calculate total width and height, considering all box model components:

```css
.calculated-box {
    width: calc(100% - 40px);
    height: calc(200px + 20px + 4px);
}
```

This comprehensive overview of CSS basics equips you with the knowledge to style and design web pages effectively. Experiment with these concepts to create visually appealing and responsive layouts.

5. CSS Animation

5.1 Introduction to CSS Animations

CSS animations bring web pages to life by adding dynamic and interactive elements. Let's explore the fundamentals of CSS animations.

5.1.1 Keyframe Animation Syntax

Keyframe animations define a sequence of styles to be gradually applied to an element. Here's the basic syntax:

```
@keyframes slide {
    0% {
    transform: translateX(0);
    }
    50% {
    transform: translateX(100px);
    }
    100% {
    transform: translateX(200px);
    }
}
```

In this example, the element will smoothly move from its initial position to 100px right and finally to 200px right.

5.1.2 Animation Properties (animation-name, duration, timing-function)

To apply a keyframe animation, use the animation property:

```css
.element {
    animation-name: slide;
    animation-duration: 2s;
    animation-timing-function: ease-in-out;
}
```

- animation-name: Specifies the name of the keyframe animation.
- animation-duration: Sets the time it takes for one cycle of the animation.
- animation-timing-function: Defines the pacing of the animation.

5.2 Creating Simple Transitions

CSS transitions allow smooth changes between property values. Let's explore how to implement simple transitions.

5.2.1 Transitioning Properties (color, background, width)

Specify the properties to transition and their respective durations:

```css
.transition-box {
    background-color: #3498db;
    color: #fff;
    width: 100px;
    height: 100px;
    transition: background-color 0.5s, color 0.5s, width 0.5s;
}

.transition-box:hover {
    background-color: #e74c3c;
    color: #000;
    width: 150px;
}
```

This example transitions the background color, text color, and width of a box on hover.

5.2.2 Transition Duration and Timing Functions

Control the duration and timing function of transitions:

```css
.transition-properties {
    transition-property: color, background-color;
    transition-duration: 1s;
    transition-timing-function: ease-in-out;
}


.transition-properties:hover {
    color: #27ae60;
    background-color: #f39c12;
}
```

5.3 Implementing Keyframe Animations

Let's dive deeper into keyframe animations and explore additional features.

5.3.1 Defining Keyframes for Custom Animations

Create more complex animations by defining keyframes:

```css
@keyframes rotateAndScale {
    0% {
    transform: rotate(0deg) scale(1);
    }
    50% {
    transform: rotate(180deg) scale(1.5);
    }
    100% {
    transform: rotate(360deg) scale(1);
    }
}
.custom-animation {
    animation: rotateAndScale 3s infinite;
}
```

In this example, an element will rotate and scale in a loop.

5.3.2 Animation Delay and Iteration

Introduce delays and control the number of iterations:

```
.delayed-animation {
    animation: rotateAndScale 2s ease-in-out 1s 3 alternate;
}
```

- animation-delay: Delays the start of the animation by a specified time.
- animation-iteration-count: Sets the number of times the animation cycle should run.

5.4 Responsive Animations with Media Queries

Adapt animations for different screen sizes using media queries.

5.4.1 Adjusting Animations for Different Screen Sizes

```
@media screen and (max-width: 600px) {
    .responsive-animation {
    animation: slideInMobile 1s ease-in-out infinite;
    }
}

@keyframes slideInMobile {
0% {
transform: translateX(0);
}
50% {
transform: translateX(50px);
}
100% {
transform: translateX(0);
}
}
```

This example animates an element differently on screens with a width of 600 pixels or less.

5.4.2 Creating Cross-Browser Compatible Animations

Ensure cross-browser compatibility by using vendor prefixes:

```css
.element {
    animation: rotate 2s linear infinite;
    -webkit-animation: rotate 2s linear infinite; /* Safari and Chrome */
    -moz-animation: rotate 2s linear infinite; /* Firefox */
    -o-animation: rotate 2s linear infinite; /* Opera */
    -ms-animation: rotate 2s linear infinite; /* Internet Explorer */
}

@keyframes rotate {
0% {
transform: rotate(0deg);
}
100% {
transform: rotate(360deg);
}
}
```

Vendor prefixes help ensure animations work smoothly across various browsers. By mastering CSS animations and transitions, you can create engaging and responsive user interfaces that enhance the user experience on your website. Experiment with different properties, durations, and timing functions to achieve the desired visual

6. HTML EDM (Email Direct Marketing)

6.1 Introduction to HTML Emails

6.1.1 Challenges and Best Practices

Email Direct Marketing (EDM) presents unique challenges and opportunities. Understanding these is crucial for effective email campaigns.

- Challenges:
  - Cross-Client Compatibility: Emails must render well across various email clients, each with its own rendering quirks.
  - Limited Design Options: Unlike web pages, emails have limited support for modern CSS and JavaScript.
  - Spam Filters: Avoiding spam filters requires careful content and structure planning.
- Best Practices:
  - Responsive Design: Craft emails with a mobile-first approach to ensure readability on different devices.
  - Simple Layouts: Keep layouts straightforward, focusing on a single column for better compatibility.
  - Clear Call-to-Action: Encourage user interaction with a clear and compelling call-to-action.

6.1.2 Inline Styles and Email Clients Compatibility

To address email client limitations, inline styles are preferred over external or internal stylesheets. This ensures consistent rendering across clients.

```html
<!DOCTYPE html>
<html lang="en">
<head>
 <title>Email Template</title>
</head>
<body style="font-family: 'Arial', sans-serif; background-color: #f2f2f2;
    color: #333; text-align: center; padding: 20px;">
 <h1 style="color: #007BFF;">Newsletter</h1>
 <p style="font-size: 16px; line-height: 1.6;">Stay updated with our
latest news and offers!</p>
 <a href="https://example.com" style="display: inline-block; ">Read
More</a>
</body>
</html>
```

6.2 Designing Responsive Email Templates

6.2.1 Fluid Layouts and Media Queries

Create responsive email templates using fluid layouts and media queries. Adjust styles based on screen size to enhance the user experience.

```
<style>
 body {
 width: 100% !important;
 margin: 0 !important;
 padding: 0 !important;
 }


 @media only screen and (max-width: 600px) {
 /* Adjust styles for smaller screens */
 body {
 font-size: 14px !important;
 }
 }
</style>
```

6.2.2 Optimizing Images for Emails

Optimize images for faster loading times and better email deliverability. Use compressed and appropriately sized images.

```
<img src="image.jpg" alt="Email Image" style="max-width: 100%; height:
auto; display: block; margin: 0 auto;">
```

6.2.3 Testing and Debugging Across Email Clients

Regularly test and debug your email templates across various email clients using tools like Litmus or Email on Acid. Address issues to ensure a consistent experience.

6.3 Crafting Engaging Email Content

6.3.1 Writing Compelling Subject Lines and Copy

Grab the reader's attention with compelling subject lines and copy. Keep it concise, relevant, and aligned with the recipient's interests.

```
Subject: Unlock Exclusive Deals Inside!
```

6.3.2 Adding Interactive Elements (Buttons, Links)

Enhance engagement by incorporating interactive elements such as buttons and links. Ensure they are easy to click on both desktop and mobile.

```
<a href="https://example.com" style="display: inline-block; padding:
10px 20px; background-color: #007BFF; color: #fff; text-decoration:
none;
border-radius: 5px;">Shop Now</a>
```

6.3.3 Using GIFs and Cinemagraphs in Emails

Capture attention with dynamic content using GIFs or cinemagraphs. Ensure they are relevant and enhance the message.

```
<img src="animated.gif" alt="Animated Image" style="max-width: 100%;
height: auto; display: block; margin: 0 auto;">
```

6.4 Email Marketing Best Practices

6.4.1 Building and Segmenting Email Lists

Build and segment email lists for targeted campaigns. Personalize content based on user preferences and behaviors.

```html
<!-- Example segmentation for a newsletter -->
<body data-category="Fashion">
 <!-- Content specific to the Fashion category -->
</body>
```

6.4.2 A/B Testing Email Campaigns

Optimize campaign performance by conducting A/B tests. Test different subject lines, content, or calls-to-action to identify the most effective elements.

```html
<!-- A/B testing two different subject lines -->
Subject: A: Exclusive Offer Inside! 
```

6.4.3 Analyzing Email Metrics and Engagement

Track and analyze email metrics, including open rates, click-through rates, and conversions. Use insights to refine future campaigns.

Effective HTML EDM practices involve a balance between creative design, responsive layouts, and compelling content. Regular testing, optimization, and analysis are key to successful email marketing campaigns.

7. Advanced CSS

7.1 Flexbox Layout

7.1.1 Introduction to Flexbox

7.1.1.1 Understanding the Flexible Box Model

Flexbox, or the Flexible Box Layout, is a powerful CSS layout model designed for building complex and responsive web layouts. It introduces a flexible box model that allows you to design dynamic and adaptive user interfaces.

7.1.1.2 Main Concepts: Flex Container and Flex Items

In flexbox, you have a flex container that holds a collection of flex items. The flex container can be a parent element, and its direct children become flex items. This allows for easy arrangement and alignment of elements.

```css
/* Creating a flex container */
.container {
    display: flex;
}


/* Styling flex items */
.item {
  flex: 1; /* Flexible and takes available space */
}
```

7.1.2 Flex Properties

7.1.2.1 flex-direction: Controlling the Direction of the Main Axis

The flex-direction property determines the primary axis of the flex container, which can be horizontal or vertical.

```css
.container {
    flex-direction: row; /* Default: left to right */
}
```

7.1.2.2 flex-wrap: Managing Item Wrapping Behavior

Use flex-wrap to control whether flex items should wrap onto multiple lines or stay on a single line.

```css
.container {
    flex-wrap: wrap; /* Allows items to wrap onto the next line */
}
```

7.1.2.3 justify-content: Aligning Items Along the Main Axis

justify-content aligns items along the main axis. Options include centering, spacing, and distributing items.

```css
.container {
    justify-content: space-between; /* Distributes items with space between them */
}
```

7.1.2.4 align-items: Aligning Items Along the Cross Axis

Align items along the cross axis using align-items. Common values include flex-start, center, and flex-end.

```css
.container {
    align-items: center; /* Align items at the center along the cross axis */
}
```

7.1.2.5 align-self: Individually Aligning Specific Items

align-self overrides the align-items property for specific flex items.

```css
.item {
    align-self: flex-end; /* Align this item at the end along the cross
axis */
}
```

7.1.3 Responsive Design with Flexbox

7.1.3.1 Adapting Layouts for Different Screen Sizes

Flexbox is inherently responsive, but you can enhance responsiveness with media queries to adjust layouts based on screen sizes.

```css
@media screen and (max-width: 600px) {
    .container {
    flex-direction: column; /* Change to a column layout on smaller
screens */
    }
}
```

7.1.3.2 Media Queries and Flexbox for Responsive Design

Combine media queries with flexbox to create responsive designs that adapt to various devices and screen sizes.

```css
@media screen and (max-width: 768px) {
    .container {
    flex-direction: column;
    }
}
```

7.2 CSS Grid

7.2.1 Introduction to CSS Grid

7.2.1.1 Overview of the Grid Layout System

CSS Grid provides a two-dimensional layout system, allowing you to define rows and columns for precise control over your web layout.

7.2.1.2 Defining Grid Containers and Grid Items

```css
/* Creating a grid container with three columns */
.container {
    display: grid;
    grid-template-columns: 1fr 1fr 1fr;
}

/* Styling grid items */
.item {
    grid-column: span 2; /* Each item spans two columns */
}
```

7.2.2 Grid Properties

7.2.2.1 grid-template-columns and grid-template-rows: Setting Column and Row Sizes

Define the size of columns and rows using grid-template-columns and grid-template-rows.

```css
.container {
    grid-template-columns: 100px 200px auto; /* Three columns with
specified sizes */
}
```

7.2.2.2 grid-gap and grid-template-areas: Controlling the Layout Structure

Use grid-gap to set the gap between grid items, and grid-template-areas to define named grid areas.

```css
.container {
    grid-gap: 10px; /* Sets a 10px gap between grid items */
}


.item {
    grid-area: header; /* Places this item in the 'header' named area */
}
```

7.2.2.3 justify-items and align-items: Aligning Items Within the Grid

Control the alignment of items within the grid using justify-items and align-items.

```css
.container {
    justify-items: center; /* Centers items along the row axis */
    align-items: end; /* Aligns items at the end along the column axis
*/
}
```

7.2.3 Responsive Design with CSS Grid

7.2.3.1 Utilizing Grid for Responsive Layouts

CSS Grid simplifies responsive design. Adjust column and row sizes based on screen width for seamless responsiveness.

```css
@media screen and (max-width: 600px) {
    .container {
    grid-template-columns: 1fr; /* Single column layout on smaller
screens */
    }
}
```

7.2.3.2 Responsive Breakpoints and Grid Adjustments

Define responsive breakpoints and adjust grid layouts accordingly for a fluid and adaptive design.

```
@media screen and (max-width: 768px) {
    .container {
    grid-template-columns: auto auto; /*Two columns on medium-sized
screens */
    }
    }
```

7.3 Transitions and Animations

7.3.1 CSS Transitions

7.3.1.1 Adding Smooth Transitions Between Property Changes

CSS transitions enable smooth property changes. Define transition properties for a subtle effect.

```
.element {
transition: background-color 0.3s ease-in-out; /* Smooth transition for
background color */
}


.element:hover {
background-color: #3498db; /* Background color change on hover */
}
```

7.3.1.2 Transition Properties: transition-property, transition-duration, transition-timing-function, transition-delay

```css
.element {
    transition-property: opacity;
    transition-duration: 1s;
    transition-timing-function: ease-in-out;
    transition-delay: 0.5s;
}


.element:hover {
    opacity: 0.5; /* Opacity change with a smooth transition on hover */
}
```

7.3.2 CSS Animations

7.3.2.1 Creating Keyframe Animations

Keyframe animations provide more control over the animation process. Define keyframes for custom animations.

```css
@keyframes slideIn {
    from {
    transform: translateX(-100%);
    }
    to {
    transform: translateX(0);
    }
}
```

8. Responsive Design with Flexbox and Grid

8.1 Mastering Flexbox Layout

8.1.1 Advanced Flexbox Techniques

8.1.1.1 Nested Flex Containers

Harness the power of nested flex containers to create intricate and adaptable layouts.

```css
/* Parent flex container */
.container {
    display: flex;
}

/* Child flex container within the parent */
.sub-container {
    display: flex;
    flex-direction: column;
}
```

Nested flex containers enable you to control the layout of child elements independently, providing a higher level of flexibility.

8.1.1.2 Flexbox for Alignment Challenges

Address alignment challenges by leveraging advanced flexbox techniques.

```css
.container {
    display: flex;
    align-items: center;
    justify-content: space-between;
}


.item {
    align-self: flex-end;
}
```

Fine-tune alignment using properties like align-self and justify-content to meet specific design requirements.

8.2 Exploring CSS Grid for Responsive Design

8.2.1 Grid Layout Strategies

8.2.1.1 Responsive Grid Design Patterns

Implement responsive grid design patterns to achieve visually appealing and adaptable layouts.

```css
/* Responsive grid with auto-sized columns */
.container {
    display: grid;
    grid-template-columns: repeat(auto-fit, minmax(200px, 1fr));
    grid-gap: 20px;
}
```

The auto-fit and minmax combination creates a grid that adjusts to the available space while maintaining a minimum and maximum column size.

8.2.1.2 Fractional Units and Responsive Sizing

Utilize fractional units to create responsive grids that adapt to different screen sizes.

```
/* Responsive grid with fractional units */
.container {
    display: grid;
    grid-template-columns: 1fr 2fr 1fr;
    grid-gap: 10px;
}
```

Fractional units distribute available space proportionally, enabling a flexible and responsive layout.

8.3 Combining Flexbox and Grid for Complex Layouts

8.3.1 Hybrid Layouts

8.3.1.1 Integrating Flexbox and Grid for Complex Designs

Combine the strengths of both flexbox and grid to achieve sophisticated and intricate layouts.

```
/* Hybrid layout using flexbox and grid */
.container {
    display: grid;
    grid-template-columns: 1fr 2fr;
}

.item {
    display: flex;
    flex-direction: column;
    justify-content: space-between;
}
```

Integrating flexbox within grid items allows for fine-tuned control over their internal structure.

8.3.1.2 Real-world Examples of Combined Layout Techniques

Explore real-world examples demonstrating the effectiveness of combining flexbox and grid for complex layouts.

```css
/* Real-world example: combining flexbox and grid */
.container {
  display: grid;
  grid-template-columns: repeat(auto-fit, minmax(300px, 1fr));
  grid-gap: 20px;
}

.item {
  display: flex;
  flex-direction: column;
  align-items: center;
}
```

In this example, a grid adapts its columns based on available space, while flexbox within each item ensures vertical alignment and centering.

By mastering the intricacies of flexbox and grid, web developers can create responsive designs that seamlessly adapt to various screen sizes and complexities. Whether used independently or in tandem, these layout techniques empower developers to build modern and visually appealing user interfaces.

9. CSS Variables

9.1 Basics of CSS Variables

9.1.1 Introduction to CSS Variables

9.1.1.1 Syntax and Declaration of Variables

CSS Variables, also known as Custom Properties, introduce a new level of flexibility and maintainability to stylesheets. They are defined using the -- prefix and can be used throughout the stylesheet.

```css
/* Declaration of CSS Variables */
:root {
    --primary-color: #3498db;
    --font-size: 16px;
}


/* Using CSS Variables in styles */
.element {
color: var(--primary-color);
font-size: var(--font-size);
}
```

Defining variables in the :root selector makes them globally accessible throughout the document.

9.1.1.2 Scope and Inheritance of Variables

CSS Variables follow the same scope and inheritance rules as other CSS properties. They inherit values from their parent elements, creating a cascading effect.

```css
.container {
    --background-color: #f2f2f2;
  }


  .element {
    background-color: var(--background-color); /* Inherits the variable
from the parent container */
  }
```

9.2 Dynamic Styling with Variables

9.2.1 Using Variables for Dynamic Styling

9.2.1.1 Changing Variable Values Dynamically with JavaScript

Leverage JavaScript to dynamically update CSS variable values, allowing for dynamic styling changes.

```html
<!DOCTYPE html>
<html lang="en"><head>
 <style>
 :root {
 --primary-color: #3498db;
 }
 .element {color: var(--primary-color);}
 </style></head><body>
 <div class="element">Dynamic Styling</div>
 <script>
 document.documentElement.style.setProperty('--primary-color',
'#e74c3c');
 </script>
</body>
</html>
```

By manipulating the CSS variables through JavaScript, developers can create dynamic user interfaces with minimal effort.

9.2.1.2 Creating Dynamic and Theme-Aware Styles

Use CSS variables to create dynamic styles that adapt to user preferences or changing application states.

```css
:root {
    --background-color: #f2f2f2;
    --text-color: #333;
}


body {
  background-color: var(--background-color);
  color: var(--text-color);
}


/* Dark theme */
.dark-theme {
    --background-color: #222;
    --text-color: #fff;
}
```

By adjusting the values of CSS variables based on user interactions or application states, developers can create dynamic and theme-aware styles.

9.3 Theming with CSS Variables

9.3.1 Theming Strategies

9.3.1.1 Implementing Theming with CSS Variables

CSS variables offer an efficient way to implement theming in web applications, making it easy to switch between different themes.

```css
:root {
--primary-color: #3498db;
}

body {
background-color: var(--primary-color);
color: #fff;
}

/* Dark theme */
.dark-theme {
--primary-color: #2c3e50;
}
```

By adjusting the values of key variables, such as --primary-color, themes can be easily implemented and switched.

9.3.1.2 Switching Between Different Themes Dynamically

Implement a dynamic theme switcher using CSS variables and JavaScript.

```html
<!DOCTYPE html>
<html lang="en">
<head>
 <style>
 :root {
 --primary-color: #3498db;
 }


 body {
 background-color: var(--primary-color);
 color: #fff;
 transition: background-color 0.3s ease;
 }


 .dark-theme {
 --primary-color: #2c3e50;
 }
 </style>
</head>
<body>

 <button onclick="toggleTheme()">Toggle Theme</button>

 <script>
 function toggleTheme() {
 document.documentElement.classList.toggle('dark-theme');
 }
 </script>

</body>
</html>
```

By toggling a class on the :root element, the theme dynamically updates, showcasing the power and flexibility of CSS variables in theming strategies.
CSS variables provide a powerful mechanism for creating maintainable and dynamic stylesheets. Whether used for basic styling or advanced theming, understanding the basics of CSS variables and their application in dynamic styling and theming scenarios is crucial for modern web development.

10. Web Performance Optimization

10.1 Minification and Compression

10.1.1 Minification Techniques

10.1.1.1 Minifying HTML, CSS, and JavaScript Files

Minification is the process of removing unnecessary characters and whitespace from code to reduce file sizes, improving loading times.

HTML Minification:

```
<!-- Before Minification -->
<!DOCTYPE html>
<html>
<head>
 <title>My Website</title>
</head>
<body>
 <p>Hello, World!</p>
</body>
</html>


<!-- After Minification -->
<!DOCTYPE html><html><head><title>My
Website</title></head><body><p>Hello, World!</p></body></html>
```

CSS Minification:

```
/* Before Minification */
body {
    font-family: 'Arial', sans-serif;
    margin: 0;
    padding: 0;
    }

/* After Minification */
    body{font-family:'Arial',sans-serif;margin:0;padding:0;}
```

JavaScript Minification:

```
// Before Minification
function sayHello() {
 console.log("Hello, World!");
}


// After Minification
function sayHello(){console.log("Hello, World!");}
```

10.1.1.2 Reducing File Size Through Code Optimization

Optimize code for performance by removing redundant code, utilizing shorthand notations, and choosing efficient algorithms.

```
/* Code Optimization in CSS */
/* Before Optimization */
div {
    margin-top: 10px;
    margin-right: 20px;
    margin-bottom: 10px;
    margin-left: 20px;
}


    /* After Optimization */
    div {margin: 10px 20px;}


    /* Code Optimization in JavaScript */
    // Before Optimization
    let result = 0;
    for (let i = 0; i < array.length; i++) {
     result += array[i];
    }


    // After Optimization
    const result = array.reduce((sum, value) => sum + value, 0);
```

10.1.2 Compression Methods

10.1.2.1 Gzip and Brotli Compression for Faster File Transfer

Compression reduces file sizes for faster data transfer between the server and the client. Gzip and Brotli are common compression methods.
Apache Gzip Configuration:

```
<IfModule mod_deflate.c>
AddOutputFilterByType DEFLATE text/plain text/html text/xml
AddOutputFilterByType DEFLATE text/css
AddOutputFilterByType DEFLATE application/javascript
AddOutputFilterByType DEFLATE application/json
AddOutputFilterByType DEFLATE application/xml
</IfModule>

Nginx Gzip Configuration:
nginx
Copy code
gzip on;
gzip_types text/plain text/html text/xml;
gzip_types text/css;
gzip_types application/javascript;
gzip_types application/json;
gzip_types application/xml;


Brotli Configuration:
nginx
Copy code
brotli on;
brotli_types text/plain text/html text/xml;
brotli_types text/css;
brotli_types application/javascript;
brotli_types application/json;
brotli_types application/xml;
```

10.2 Lazy Loading Images

10.2.1 Image Lazy Loading

10.2.1.1 Delaying the Loading of Images Until They Are Needed
Lazy loading defers the loading of images until they are about to be displayed, reducing initial page load times.

```
Before Lazy Loading:
<!-- Before Lazy Loading -->
<img src="image.jpg" alt="A Beautiful Image">

After Lazy Loading:
<!-- After Lazy Loading -->
<img data-src="image.jpg" alt="A Beautiful Image" loading="lazy">
```

10.2.1.2 Improving Page Load Speed and Performance
Lazy loading improves performance by prioritizing the loading of visible content, reducing unnecessary image requests on initial page load.

10.3 Critical Rendering Path Optimization

10.3.1 Optimizing the Critical Rendering Path

10.3.1.1 Prioritizing and Optimizing Critical Resources
Optimize the critical rendering path by prioritizing essential resources such as CSS, JavaScript, and visible content.

```
<!-- Before Optimization -->
<head>
 <link rel="stylesheet" href="styles.css">
 <script src="app.js"></script>
</head>
<!-- After Optimization -->
<head>
 <link rel="preload" href="styles.css" as="style"
onload="this.rel='stylesheet'">
 <script src="app.js" defer></script>
</head>
```

10.3.1.2 Improving Time to First Paint and Overall Rendering Performance

Improve time to first paint by minimizing render-blocking resources, deferring non-critical scripts, and optimizing the order of resource loading.

```html
<!-- Before Optimization -->
<head>
 <link rel="stylesheet" href="styles.css">
 <script src="non_critical.js"></script>
</head>

<!-- After Optimization -->
<head>
 <link rel="preload" href="styles.css" as="style"
onload="this.rel='stylesheet'">
 <script src="non_critical.js" defer></script>
</head>
```

By applying minification, compression, lazy loading, and optimizing the critical rendering path, web developers can significantly enhance web performance, reduce page load times, and provide a better user experience.

11. Web Performance Optimization

Web performance optimization is crucial for delivering a fast and responsive user experience. In this chapter, we will explore key strategies to enhance the performance of web applications.

11.1 Minification and Compression

11.1.1 Minification Techniques

Minification involves reducing the size of HTML, CSS, and JavaScript files by removing unnecessary characters and whitespace.

11.1.1.1 Minifying HTML, CSS, and JavaScript Files

Minification improves load times by reducing file sizes:

HTML

```
<!-- HTML Before Minification -->
<!DOCTYPE html>
<html>
<head>
 <title>My Website</title>
</head>
<body>
 <p>Hello, World!</p>
</body>
</html>


<!-- After Minification -->
<!DOCTYPE html><html><head><title>My
Website</title></head><body><p>Hello, World!</p></body></html>
```

css

```css
/* css Before Minification */
body {
    font-family: 'Arial', sans-serif;
    margin: 0;
    padding: 0;
}


/* After Minification */
body{font-family:'Arial',sans-serif;margin:0;padding:0;}
```

javascript

```javascript
// javascript Before Minification
function sayHello() {
    console.log("Hello, World!");
}


// After Minification
function sayHello(){console.log("Hello, World!");}
```

11.1.1.2 Reducing File Size Through Code Optimization

Optimize code for performance by removing redundancy and using efficient algorithms:

```css
/* Code Optimization in CSS */
/* Before Optimization */
div {
    margin-top: 10px;
    margin-right: 20px;
    margin-bottom: 10px;
    margin-left: 20px;
}


/* After Optimization */
div {margin: 10px 20px;}
```

```
/* Code Optimization in JavaScript */
// Before Optimization
let result = 0;
for (let i = 0; i < array.length; i++) {
 result += array[i];
}


// After Optimization
const result = array.reduce((sum, value) => sum + value, 0);
```

11.1.2 Compression Methods

11.1.2.1 Gzip and Brotli Compression for Faster File Transfer

Use compression to further reduce file sizes during transfer:
Apache Gzip Configuration:

```
<IfModule mod_deflate.c>
 AddOutputFilterByType DEFLATE text/plain text/html text/xml
 AddOutputFilterByType DEFLATE text/css
 AddOutputFilterByType DEFLATE application/javascript
 AddOutputFilterByType DEFLATE application/json
 AddOutputFilterByType DEFLATE application/xml
</IfModule>

Nginx Gzip Configuration:
nginx
Copy code
gzip on;
gzip_types text/plain text/html text/xml;
gzip_types text/css;
gzip_types application/javascript;
gzip_types application/json;
gzip_types application/xml;
```

```
    Brotli Configuration:
nginx
Copy code
brotli on;
brotli_types text/plain text/html text/xml;
brotli_types text/css;
brotli_types application/javascript;
brotli_types application/json;
brotli_types application/xml;
```

11.2 Lazy Loading Images

11.2.1 Image Lazy Loading

11.2.1.1 Delaying the Loading of Images Until They Are Needed

Implement lazy loading to defer the loading of images until they are about to be displayed:

Before Lazy Loading:

```html
<!-- Before Lazy Loading -->
<img src="image.jpg" alt="A Beautiful Image">
```

After Lazy Loading:

```html
<!-- After Lazy Loading -->
<img data-src="image.jpg" alt="A Beautiful Image" loading="lazy">
```

11.2.1.2 Improving Page Load Speed and Performance

Lazy loading improves initial page load times by prioritizing the loading of visible content:

11.3 Critical Rendering Path Optimization

11.3.1 Optimizing the Critical Rendering Path

11.3.1.1 Prioritizing and Optimizing Critical Resources

Optimize the critical rendering path by prioritizing essential resources such as CSS and JavaScript:

```html
<!-- Before Optimization -->
<head>
  <link rel="stylesheet" href="styles.css">
  <script src="app.js"></script>
</head>


<!-- After Optimization -->
<head>
  <link rel="preload" href="styles.css" as="style"
onload="this.rel='stylesheet'">
  <script src="app.js" defer></script>
</head>
```

11.3.1.2 Improving Time to First Paint and Overall Rendering Performance

Improve time to first paint by minimizing render-blocking resources:

```html
<!-- Before Optimization -->
<head>
 <link rel="stylesheet" href="styles.css">
 <script src="non_critical.js"></script>
</head>


<!-- After Optimization -->
<head>
 <link rel="preload" href="styles.css" as="style"
onload="this.rel='stylesheet'">
 <script src="non_critical.js" defer></script>
</head>
```

By implementing these performance optimization techniques, web developers can significantly enhance the speed and responsiveness of web applications, providing users with a seamless and enjoyable browsing experience.

12. JavaScript Basics

JavaScript serves as a fundamental building block for web development, empowering developers to create dynamic and interactive experiences. Let's delve into the core aspects of JavaScript.

12.1 Basics of JavaScript

JavaScript is a versatile scripting language primarily used for web development. It enables the creation of dynamic and interactive content within web pages. Here's a brief overview of its key features:

- Client-Side Scripting: JavaScript executes on the client's browser, enhancing user interfaces and enabling real-time interactions.
- Object-Oriented: JavaScript supports object-oriented programming principles, allowing the creation and manipulation of objects.
- Event-Driven: Interactivity is achieved through event-driven programming, responding to user actions like clicks and keystrokes.

12.2 Variables, Data Types, and Operators

In JavaScript, variables store data, and understanding data types is crucial for effective programming. Operators perform operations on variables and values. Let's look at a quick example:

```javascript
// Variable Declaration and Initialization
let greeting = "Hello,";
let name = "John";

// Concatenation using the + Operator
let message = greeting + " " + name;

// Displaying the Result
console.log(message); // Outputs: Hello, John
```

In this example, let declares variables, "Hello," and "John" are strings, and the + operator concatenates them.

12.3 Control Flow and Loops

Control flow structures dictate the order in which statements are executed. Loops allow for the repeated execution of code. Consider the following example:

```javascript
// Control Flow with if-else Statement
let age = 25;

if (age >= 18) {
  console.log("You are an adult.");
} else {
  console.log("You are a minor.");
}


// Looping with for Loop
for (let i = 1; i <= 5; i++) {
  console.log("Iteration " + i);
}
```

In this snippet, an if-else statement checks if a person is an adult based on their age, and a for loop iterates five times, displaying the current iteration.

Mastering these JavaScript basics provides a solid foundation for creating dynamic and interactive web applications. The next step is to explore more advanced concepts, such as functions, objects, and asynchronous programming, to enhance your JavaScript skills further.

13. JavaScript Functions

13.1 Declaring and Invoking Functions

Functions in JavaScript are blocks of reusable code. Declaring a function involves defining its structure, and invoking it executes the code within.

```javascript
// Function Declaration
function greet(name) {
    console.log("Hello, " + name + "!");
}


// Function Invocation
greet("John");
```

13.2 Function Parameters and Return Values

13.2.1 Default Parameters

Assign default values to function parameters, ensuring they have a value even if not explicitly provided during the function call.

```javascript
function greet(name = "Guest") {
console.log("Hello, " + name + "!");
}

greet(); // Outputs: Hello, Guest!
```

13.2.2 Rest Parameters

Use the rest parameter to capture multiple arguments into an array, providing flexibility in the number of parameters a function can accept.

```javascript
function sum(...numbers) {
    return numbers.reduce((total, num) => total + num, 0);
}

const result = sum(1, 2, 3, 4, 5);
console.log(result); // Outputs: 15
```

13.3 Scope and Closures

13.3.1 Lexical Scope

JavaScript uses lexical (static) scope, meaning the scope of a variable is determined by its location within the source code.

```javascript
function outer() {
    const message = "Hello, ";

    function inner(name) {
    console.log(message + name);
    }

    return inner;
}

const greetFunction = outer();
greetFunction("John"); // Outputs: Hello, John
```

13.3.2 Closure Patterns

Closures occur when a function is defined inside another function, allowing access to the outer function's variables. Common closure patterns include the module pattern and the factory function pattern.

module pattern :

```javascript
// Module Pattern
const counter = (function() {
    let count = 0;
    return {
    increment: function() {
    count++;
    },
    getCount: function() {
    return count;
    }
    };
})();
counter.increment();
console.log(counter.getCount()); // Outputs: 1
```

factory function pattern :

```javascript
// Factory Function Pattern
function createPerson(name) {
    let age = 0;

    return {
    getName: function() {
    return name;
    },
    getAge: function() {
    return age;
    },
    increaseAge: function() {
    age++;
    }
    };
}

const person = createPerson("Alice");
person.increaseAge();
console.log(person.getAge()); // Outputs: 1
```

Understanding JavaScript functions, including parameter handling, scope, and closures, lays the foundation for building robust and modular applications. These concepts are essential for writing efficient and maintainable JavaScript code.

14. Arrays in JavaScript

Arrays in JavaScript are versatile and powerful data structures that allow you to store and manipulate collections of elements. Let's explore various aspects of working with arrays, including their introduction, common methods, and multi-dimensional arrays.

14.1 Introduction to Arrays

Arrays are ordered, indexed collections of values in JavaScript. They can hold various data types, including numbers, strings, and objects. Here's a basic example of creating an array:

```javascript
// Creating an Array
let fruits = ["Apple", "Banana", "Orange", "Mango"];


// Accessing Array Elements
console.log(fruits[0]); // Outputs: Apple
console.log(fruits[2]); // Outputs: Orange
```

Arrays are indexed starting from 0, and you can access elements using square brackets and the index.

14.2 Array Methods: forEach, map, filter, reduce

JavaScript provides powerful array methods that simplify common operations on arrays. Let's explore some of the key methods:

14.2.1 The forEach Method

The forEach method iterates over each element in the array and executes a provided function for each.

```javascript
// Using forEach to Log Array Elements
fruits.forEach(function (fruit) {
    console.log(fruit);
});
// Outputs:
// Apple
// Banana
// Orange
// Mango
```

14.2.2 The map Method

The map method creates a new array by applying a function to each element of the original array.

```javascript
// Using map to Create a New Array
let fruitLengths = fruits.map(function (fruit) {
    return fruit.length;
});
console.log(fruitLengths); // Outputs: [5, 6, 6, 5]
```

14.2.3 The filter Method

The filter method creates a new array containing elements that pass a certain condition.

```javascript
// Using filter to Get Fruits with Length Greater Than 5
let longFruits = fruits.filter(function (fruit) {
    return fruit.length > 5;
});
console.log(longFruits); // Outputs: ["Banana", "Orange"]
```

14.2.4 The reduce Method

The reduce method reduces the array to a single value by executing a provided function for each element.

```javascript
// Using reduce to Get Total Length of Fruits
let totalLength = fruits.reduce(function (accumulator, fruit) {
    return accumulator + fruit.length;
}, 0);
console.log(totalLength); // Outputs: 22
```

14.3 Working with Multi-dimensional Arrays

14.3.1 Creating and Accessing 2D Arrays

A 2D array is an array of arrays. It can be created to represent a table or grid structure.

```javascript
// Creating a 2D Array
let matrix = [
    [1, 2, 3],
    [4, 5, 6],
    [7, 8, 9]
];


// Accessing Elements in a 2D Array
console.log(matrix[0][1]); // Outputs: 2
console.log(matrix[2][2]); // Outputs: 9
```

14.3.2 Operations on Multi-dimensional Arrays

Performing operations on multi-dimensional arrays involves nested loops.

```javascript
// Summing all Elements in a 2D Array
let sum = 0;
for (let row = 0; row < matrix.length; row++) {
  for (let col = 0; col < matrix[row].length; col++) {
  sum += matrix[row][col];
  }
}
console.log(sum); // Outputs: 45
```

Working with multi-dimensional arrays is common when dealing with grid-based data, such as images or game boards.

Understanding array methods and multi-dimensional arrays provides the tools needed to efficiently manipulate and process data in JavaScript. These skills are essential for building complex applications and handling diverse datasets.

15. Objects in JavaScript

Objects in JavaScript are fundamental data structures that enable the organization and manipulation of data. Let's explore the introduction to objects, creating and manipulating them, object methods and prototypes, and object destructuring with spread syntax.

15.1 Introduction to Objects

An object in JavaScript is a collection of key-value pairs where each key is a string and each value can be any data type, including other objects. Objects are versatile and provide a way to structure and represent complex data.

```javascript
// Creating an Object
let person = {
    firstName: "John",
    lastName: "Doe",
    age: 30,
    isStudent: false,
    address: {
    city: "New York",
    zipCode: "10001"
    }
};

// Accessing Object Properties
console.log(person.firstName); // Outputs: John
console.log(person.address.city); // Outputs: New York
```

15.2 Creating and Manipulating Objects

Objects can be created using object literals or the Object constructor. Properties can be added, modified, or deleted dynamically.

```javascript
// Creating Objects
let car = { brand: "Toyota", model: "Camry" };
let laptop = new Object();
laptop.brand = "Dell";
laptop.model = "XPS";

// Modifying Object Properties
car.model = "Corolla";

// Deleting Object Properties
delete car.brand;

// Checking if a Property Exists
console.log("brand" in car); // Outputs: false
```

15.3 Object Methods and Prototypes

15.3.1 Adding Methods to Objects

Methods are functions stored as object properties. They can perform operations related to the object.

```javascript
// Adding a Method to an Object
let calculator = {
    add: function (a, b) {
    return a + b;
    },
    subtract: function (a, b) {
    return a - b;
    }
};

    // Using Object Method
    console.log(calculator.add(5, 3)); // Outputs: 8
```

15.3.2 Understanding Prototypes

Prototypes allow objects to inherit properties and methods from other objects, creating a prototype chain.

```javascript
// Creating a Prototype Object
let vehicle = {
    type: "Car",
    drive: function () {
    console.log("Vroom!");
    }
};

// Creating an Object with a Prototype
let myCar = Object.create(vehicle);
myCar.brand = "Honda";

// Accessing Inherited Method
myCar.drive(); // Outputs: Vroom!
```

15.4 Object Destructuring and Spread Syntax

15.4.1 Destructuring Objects

Destructuring allows extracting values from objects and assigning them to variables easily.

```javascript
// Destructuring Object
let { firstName, lastName } = person;
console.log(firstName, lastName); // Outputs: John Doe
```

15.4.2 Spreading Objects

Spread syntax allows creating copies of objects or merging multiple objects into one.

```javascript
// Spreading Objects
let laptopSpecs = { RAM: "8GB", storage: "256GB SSD" };
let updatedLaptop = { ...laptop, ...laptopSpecs };
console.log(updatedLaptop); // Outputs: { brand: "Dell", model: "XPS", RAM: "8GB", storage: "256GB SSD" }
```

Understanding objects, their methods, prototypes, and advanced features like destructuring and spread syntax is crucial for effective JavaScript development. Objects provide a flexible and powerful way to structure and organize data in your applications.

16. JavaScript and Asynchronous Programming

16.1 Introduction to Asynchronous Programming

Asynchronous programming allows non-blocking execution of code, enabling tasks to run concurrently without waiting for each other to complete. It's crucial for handling time-consuming operations, such as network requests or file I/O, without freezing the application.

16.2 Callbacks, Promises, and Async/Await

16.2.1 Callbacks

Callbacks are functions passed as arguments to another function and executed once a task is completed.

```javascript
// Example of Callback
function fetchData(callback) {
    setTimeout(() => {
    console.log("Data Fetched!");
    callback();
    }, 1000);
}

function processData() {
    console.log("Data Processed!");
}
```

16.2.2 Promises

Promises provide a cleaner approach to handle asynchronous operations, allowing chaining of multiple tasks.

```javascript
// Example of Promises
function fetchData() {
    return new Promise((resolve, reject) => {
    setTimeout(() => {
    console.log("Data Fetched!");
    resolve();
    }, 1000);
    });
}


    function processData() {
    console.log("Data Processed!");
    }


    fetchData().then(processData);
```

16.2.3 Async/Await

Async/Await simplifies working with Promises, making asynchronous code look synchronous.

```javascript
// Example of Async/Await
async function fetchData() {
    return new Promise((resolve) => {
    setTimeout(() => {
    console.log("Data Fetched!");
    resolve();
    }, 1000);
    });
}

    async function processData() {
    console.log("Data Processed!");
    }

    async function fetchDataAndProcess() {
    await fetchData();
    processData();
    }

    fetchDataAndProcess();
```

16.3 Handling AJAX Request

AJAX (Asynchronous JavaScript and XML) allows fetching data from a server without refreshing the entire page.

```javascript
// Example of AJAX with Fetch API
fetch('https://jsonplaceholder.typicode.com/todos/1')
  .then(response => response.json())
  .then(data => console.log(data))
  .catch(error => console.error('Error:', error));
```

17. JavaScript ES6+ Features

17.1 Arrow Functions

Arrow functions provide a concise syntax for writing functions.

```javascript
// Example of Arrow Function
const add = (a, b) => a + b;
console.log(add(2, 3)); // Outputs: 5
```

17.2 Destructuring

Destructuring simplifies extracting values from arrays and objects.

```javascript
// Example of Destructuring
const person = { name: "John", age: 30 };
const { name, age } = person;
console.log(name, age); // Outputs: John 30
```

17.3 Template Literals and Tagged Templates

Template literals allow embedding expressions in strings.

```javascript
// Example of Template Literals
const name = "World";
const greeting = `Hello, ${name}!`;
console.log(greeting); // Outputs: Hello, World!
```

17.4 Default Parameters and Rest/Spread Operators

Default parameters provide default values for function parameters.

```javascript
// Example of Default Parameters
function greet(name = "Guest") {
    console.log(`Hello, ${name}!`);
}


greet(); // Outputs: Hello, Guest!
```

Rest and spread operators simplify working with variable numbers of arguments.

```javascript
// Example of Rest/Spread Operators
function sum(...numbers) {
    return numbers.reduce((total, num) => total + num, 0);
}


const numbers = [1, 2, 3, 4, 5];
console.log(sum(...numbers)); // Outputs: 15
```

17.5 Let, Const, and Block Scoping

let and const provide block-scoping for variables.

```javascript
// Example of Let and Const
function example() {
    if (true) {
    let x = 10;
    const y = 20;
    }


    // console.log(x); // ReferenceError: x is not defined
    // console.log(y); // ReferenceError: y is not defined

}
```

17.6 Enhanced Object Literals

Enhanced object literals provide shorthand syntax for defining object properties.

```javascript
// Example of Enhanced Object Literals
const name = "John";
const age = 30;

const person = { name, age };
console.log(person); // Outputs: { name: 'John', age: 30 }
```

17.7 Classes and Inheritance

ES6 introduced class syntax for creating objects with a more familiar structure.

```javascript
// Example of Classes and Inheritance
class Animal {
    constructor(name) {
    this.name = name;
    }

    speak() {
    console.log(`${this.name} makes a sound.`);
    }
}

class Dog extends Animal {
    speak() {
    console.log(`${this.name} barks.`);
    }
}

const dog = new Dog('Buddy');
dog.speak(); // Outputs: Buddy barks.
```

17.8 Modules

Modules allow organizing code into separate files and exporting/importing functionality.

```javascript
// Example of Modules
// File: utils.js
export const add = (a, b) => a + b;

// File: main.js
import { add } from './utils';
console.log(add(2, 3)); // Outputs: 5
```

17.9 Maps and Sets

Maps and Sets provide data structures for key-value pairs and unique values.

```javascript
// Example of Maps and Sets
const myMap = new Map();
myMap.set('name', 'John');

const mySet = new Set([1, 2, 3, 3, 4]);
console.log([...mySet]); // Outputs: [1, 2, 3, 4]
```

17.10 Generators

Generators enable pausing and resuming the execution of a function.

```javascript
// Example of Generators
function* generator() {
    yield 1;
    yield 2;
    yield 3;
}

const gen = generator();
console.log(gen.next().value); // Outputs: 1
```

17.11 Proxies and Reflect API

Proxies allow intercepting and customizing object operations.

```javascript
// Example of Proxies and Reflect API
const handler = {
    get: function (target, prop, receiver) {
    console.log(`Getting ${prop}`);
    return Reflect.get(target, prop, receiver);
    }
};

const proxy = new Proxy({}, handler);
proxy.name; // Outputs: Getting name
```

17.12 Symbol

Symbols are unique and immutable data types often used as object keys.

```javascript
// Example of Symbol
const mySymbol = Symbol('mySymbol');
const obj = { [mySymbol]: 'Hello' };

console.log(obj[mySymbol]); // Outputs: Hello
```

17.13 Iterators and Iterables

Iterators allow custom iterations over objects.

```javascript
// Example of Iterators and Iterables
const iterable = [1, 2, 3];

const iterator = iterable[Symbol.iterator]();
console.log
```

18. Context API in React

18.1 Introduction to the Context API

The Context API in React provides a way to share values like themes or authentication status between components without explicitly passing them through each level of the component tree. It simplifies the prop-drilling problem.

18.2 Creating and Consuming Context

To use the Context API, create a context and wrap your components with it.

```jsx
// Example of Creating Context
import React, { createContext, useContext } from 'react';

const MyContext = createContext();

// Example of Providing Context
const App = () => {
 const value = 'Hello from Context!';
 return (
<MyContext.Provider value={value}>
<ChildComponent />
</MyContext.Provider>
 );
};

// Example of Consuming Context
const ChildComponent = () => {
 const contextValue = useContext(MyContext);
 return <div>{contextValue}</div>;
};
```

18.3 Context API for State Management

The Context API can also be used for state management by combining it with the useReducer hook or a state management library like Redux.

```jsx
// Example of State Management with Context API
import React, { createContext, useContext, useReducer } from 'react';

const initialState = { count: 0 };

const reducer = (state, action) => {
 switch (action.type) {
 case 'increment':
 return { count: state.count + 1 };
 default:
 return state;
 }
};

const StateContext = createContext();
const App = () => {
 const [state, dispatch] = useReducer(reducer, initialState);

 return (
 <StateContext.Provider value={{ state, dispatch }}>
 <ChildComponent />
 </StateContext.Provider>
 );
};

const ChildComponent = () => {
 const { state, dispatch } = useContext(StateContext);

 return (
 <div>
 <p>Count: {state.count}</p>
 <button onClick={() => dispatch({ type: 'increment' })}>
 Increment
 </button>
 </div>
 );
};
```

19. JavaScript Libraries for Animation

19.1 GSAP (GreenSock Animation Platform)

GSAP is a robust JavaScript animation library used for creating high-performance, smooth animations. It offers a wide range of features and is popular for its ease of use.

Installation:

Include the GSAP library in your project. You can either download it from the official website or use a package manager like npm or yarn.

```html
<!-- Include the GSAP library -->
<script src="https://unpkg.com/gsap@3.9.1/dist/gsap.min.js"></script>
```

Basic Animation Example:

```html
<!DOCTYPE html>
<html lang="en">
<head>
 <meta charset="UTF-8">
 <meta name="viewport" content="width=device-width, initial-scale=1.0">
 <title>GSAP Example</title>
</head>
<body>
 <div id="animatedElement">Hello, GSAP!</div>

 <script>
 // Create a GSAP timeline
 const tl = gsap.timeline();

 // Add an animation to the timeline
 tl.to("#animatedElement", { duration: 2, x: 200, opacity: 0.5,
rotation: 360 });
 </script>
</body>
</html>
```

In this example, GSAP is used to animate the #animatedElement div, moving it 200 pixels to the right, changing its opacity, and rotating it 360 degrees over a duration of 2 seconds.

19.2 Anime.js

Anime.js is a lightweight and flexible JavaScript animation library that enables developers to create complex and expressive animations with ease. It provides a straightforward API and powerful features, making it a popular choice for web developers seeking a modern animation solution. Anime.js is designed to work seamlessly with HTML, SVG, and CSS properties, allowing for a wide range of creative possibilities in web development.

Getting Started with Anime.js:

To use Anime.js in your web projects, follow these steps:

Installation:

Include the Anime.js library in your project. You can download it from the official website or use a package manager like npm or yarn.

```html
<!-- Include the Anime.js library -->
<script
src="https://cdn.jsdelivr.net/npm/animejs@3.2.1/lib/anime.min.js"></script>
```

Basic Animation Example:

```html
<!DOCTYPE html>
<html lang="en">
<head>
 <meta charset="UTF-8">
 <meta name="viewport" content="width=device-width, initial-scale=1.0">
 <title>Anime.js Example</title>
</head>
<body>
 <div id="animatedElement">Hello, Anime.js!</div>

 <script>
 // Create an Anime.js animation
 anime({
 targets: '#animatedElement',
 translateX: 250,
 rotate: '1turn',
 backgroundColor: '#FF5733',
 duration: 2000,
 easing: 'easeInOutQuad',
 });
 </script>
</body>
</html>
```

In this example, Anime.js is used to animate the #animatedElement div, translating it 250 pixels to the right, rotating it one turn, changing its background color, and doing so over a duration of 2 seconds with a specified easing function.

Anime.js Documentation and Resources:

For in-depth learning and exploration, refer to the official Anime.js documentation:
- Anime.js Documentation

The documentation provides comprehensive information on Anime.js features, syntax, and usage.

19.3 Using CSS for Animations

CSS can also be used for animations, especially for simpler transitions and effects. Keyframes and transition properties in CSS are commonly employed for animations.

```css
/* Example of CSS Animation */
.element {
    transition: transform 2s ease-in-out, opacity 2s ease-in-out;
}

.element:hover {
    transform: translateX(100px);
    opacity: 0.5;
}
```

Choosing an animation library depends on the project requirements and the complexity of animations needed. GSAP and Anime.js are versatile and widely used, while CSS animations are suitable for simpler cases.

20. React.js Basics

20.1 Introduction to React.js

React.js is a JavaScript library for building user interfaces, developed by Facebook. It allows developers to create reusable UI components and manage the state of applications efficiently. React follows a component-based architecture, making it easy to build and maintain complex UIs.

20.2 Components and Props

In React, components are the building blocks of the user interface. They are reusable, self-contained pieces of code responsible for rendering a part of the UI. Props (short for properties) are used to pass data from a parent component to a child component.

```javascript
// Example of React Component with Props
import React from 'react';

const Greeting = (props) => {
 return <p>Hello, {props.name}!</p>;
};


const App = () => {
 return <Greeting name="John" />;
};
```

20.3 State and Lifecycle

State allows components to manage and store data that can change over time. The useState hook is commonly used to introduce state to functional components.

```jsx
// Example of React State and Lifecycle
import React, { useState, useEffect } from 'react';

const Counter = () => {
  const [count, setCount] = useState(0);

  useEffect(() => {
    document.title = `Count: ${count}`;
  }, [count]);

  return (
    <div>
    <p>Count: {count}</p>
    <button onClick={() => setCount(count + 1)}>Increment</button>
    </div>
  );
};
```

21. Redux for State Management

21.1 Understanding Redux

Redux is a predictable state container for JavaScript applications. It provides a centralized store to manage the state of an entire application. Actions are dispatched to modify the state through reducers, ensuring a single source of truth for the application state.

21.2 Actions, Reducers, and Store

- Actions: Actions are plain JavaScript objects that describe changes in the application state. They are dispatched to trigger state modifications.

```javascript
// Example of Redux Action
const increment = () => {
    return { type: 'INCREMENT' };
};
```

- Reducers: Reducers specify how the state changes in response to actions. They are pure functions that take the current state and an action, returning the new state.

```javascript
// Example of Redux Reducer
const counterReducer = (state = { count: 0 }, action) => {
    switch (action.type) {
    case 'INCREMENT':
    return { count: state.count + 1 };
    default:
    return state;
    }
};
```

- Store: The store holds the complete state tree of the application. It can dispatch actions and notify subscribers when the state changes.

```
// Example of Redux Store
import { createStore } from 'redux';

const store = createStore(counterReducer);
```

21.3 Connecting React with Redux

The react-redux library allows React components to connect to the Redux store and access its state and dispatch actions.

```
// Example of Connecting React with Redux
import React from 'react';
import { connect } from 'react-redux';

const Counter = ({ count, increment }) => {
  return (
    <div>
      <p>Count: {count}</p>
      <button onClick={increment}>Increment</button>
    </div>
  );
};

const mapStateToProps = (state) => {
  return {
    count: state.count,
  };
};
const mapDispatchToProps = (dispatch) => {
  return {
    increment: () => dispatch({ type: 'INCREMENT' }),
  };
};

export default connect(mapStateToProps, mapDispatchToProps)(Counter);
```

22. Data Fetching with Axios

22.1 Introduction to Axios

Axios is a popular JavaScript library for making HTTP requests. It is commonly used in React applications to fetch data from APIs.

22.2 Making GET and POST Requests

Axios provides simple methods for making various types of HTTP requests.

```javascript
// Example of Axios GET Request
import axios from 'axios';

axios.get('https://jsonplaceholder.typicode.com/posts/1')
  .then(response => console.log(response.data))
  .catch(error => console.error('Error:', error));
```

```javascript
// Example of Axios POST Request
import axios from 'axios';

const postData = { title: 'New Post', body: 'This is a new post.' };

axios.post('https://jsonplaceholder.typicode.com/posts', postData)
  .then(response => console.log(response.data))
  .catch(error => console.error('Error:', error));
```

22.3 Handling Responses and Errors

Axios responses include information such as data, status, and headers. Error handling is crucial to manage failed requests.

```javascript
// Example of Handling Axios Responses and Errors
import axios from 'axios';

axios.get('https://jsonplaceholder.typicode.com/posts/1')
  .then(response => console.log(response.data))
  .catch(error => {
  if (error.response) {
  console.error('Error Response:', error.response.data);
  } else if (error.request) {
  console.error('No Response Received:', error.request);
  } else {
  console.error('Error:', error.message);
  }
});
```

Understanding React.js fundamentals, state management with Redux, and data fetching with Axios are essential skills for building robust and dynamic web applications. These concepts provide a solid foundation for more advanced development in the React ecosystem.

23. State Management with Redux Toolkit

23.1 Introduction to Redux Toolkit

Redux Toolkit is a set of utilities designed to simplify Redux development. It includes createSlice for reducer logic and state definition, configureStore for store setup, and other helpful functions. It streamlines the Redux setup process, reducing boilerplate code.

```javascript
// Example of Redux Toolkit Slice
import { createSlice } from '@reduxjs/toolkit';

const counterSlice = createSlice({
name: 'counter',
initialState: { value: 0 },
reducers: {
increment: state => {
state.value += 1;
},
decrement: state => {
state.value -= 1;
},
},
});

export const { increment, decrement } = counterSlice.actions;
export default counterSlice.reducer;
```

23.2 Slices and Immer for Immutability

Slices generated by createSlice use Immer under the hood, allowing developers to write code that looks like it's directly mutating the state, while it's producing immutable updates.

```javascript
// Example of Immer in Redux Toolkit Slice
import { createSlice } from '@reduxjs/toolkit';

const userSlice = createSlice({
  name: 'user',
  initialState: { name: 'John', age: 25 },
  reducers: {
    updateName: (state, action) => {
      state.name = action.payload; // No need for immutable update logic
    },
  },
});
```

23.3 Asynchronous Operations with Redux Toolkit

Redux Toolkit simplifies handling asynchronous operations using the createAsyncThunk function. It automatically generates action creators that dispatch pending, fulfilled, and rejected actions for async requests.

```javascript
// Example of Async Operation with Redux Toolkit
import { createSlice, createAsyncThunk } from '@reduxjs/toolkit';
import axios from 'axios';

const fetchUser = createAsyncThunk('user/fetchUser', async (userId) => {
 const response = await axios.get(`/api/users/${userId}`);
 return response.data;
});

const userSlice = createSlice({
 name: 'user',
 initialState: { data: null, status: 'idle' },
 reducers: {},
 extraReducers: (builder) => {
 builder
 .addCase(fetchUser.pending, (state) => {
 state.status = 'loading';
 })
 .addCase(fetchUser.fulfilled, (state, action) => {
 state.status = 'succeeded';
 state.data = action.payload;
 })
 .addCase(fetchUser.rejected, (state) => {
 state.status = 'failed';
 });
 },
});

export { fetchUser };
```

24. Next.js for React

24.1 Introduction to Next.js

Next.js is a React framework that simplifies the development of server-side rendered (SSR) and statically generated (SSG) React applications. It is built on top of React, providing additional features and conventions to enhance the development experience. Here are some key aspects:

- Automatic Code Splitting: Next.js automatically splits your JavaScript code into smaller chunks, optimizing the loading performance of your web application.

- Server-Side Rendering (SSR): Next.js supports SSR out of the box. This means that pages can be rendered on the server, improving initial page load times and providing a better user experience.

- Statically Generated Pages (SSG): Next.js allows you to generate static pages at build time, reducing the need for server resources during runtime. This is beneficial for content that doesn't change frequently.

24.2 Setting up a Next.js Project

Step 1: Create a Next.js Project

Open your terminal and run the following command to create a new Next.js project:

npx create-next-app my-nextjs-project

Replace my-nextjs-project with your desired project name.

Step 2: Navigate to Your Project

Change into your project directory:

cd my-nextjs-project

Step 3: Run the Development Server

Start the development server to see your initial Next.js application:

npm run dev

This command will launch the development server, and you can access your Next.js application by visiting **http://localhost:3000** in your web browser.

Step 4: Explore the Project Structure

Next.js projects come with a predefined structure. Key directories include:

Pages: This is where you create your pages. Each .js or .tsx file inside this directory becomes a route in your application.

Public: Static assets like images, fonts, or any file that doesn't need processing by webpack can be placed here.

Styles: CSS files or styles related to your application can be stored here.

Step 5: Create Your First Page

Next.js pages are automatically associated with routes. Create a new file in the pages directory, for example, pages/index.js:

```javascript
// pages/index.js
function HomePage() {
    return (
      <div>
        <h1>Welcome to Next.js!</h1>
      </div>
    );}
  export default HomePage;
```

Save the file, and you should see the changes reflected in your browser.

Step 6: Customize Configuration (Optional)

Next.js provides a wide range of configurations. For example, you can modify next.config.js to customize webpack configurations, or install additional packages for styling, state management, etc., based on your project needs.

Step 7: Build Your Application

When you are ready to deploy your application, you can build it using the following command:

npm run build

This command creates an optimized production-ready build in the out directory.

Conclusion:

You've successfully set up a basic Next.js project! This is just the starting point, and you can now begin building your application, adding components, pages, and exploring the various features that Next.js offers for server-side rendering, routing, and more. Don't forget to refer to the Next.js documentation for more in-depth information and advanced topics.

24.3 Server-Side Rendering and Routing in Next.js

Server-side rendering in Next.js is achieved through the getServerSideProps function. This function runs on the server for every request and fetches data before rendering the component.

```javascript
// Example of Server-Side Rendering in Next.js
import React from 'react';

const Page = ({ data }) => {
  return <div>{data}</div>;
};
export async function getServerSideProps() {
  // Fetch data on the server before rendering the component
  const data = await fetchData();
  return {
  props: { data },
  };
}
export default Page;
```

Next.js simplifies routing using the Link component, enabling seamless navigation between pages without the need for full-page reloads.

```javascript
// Example of Routing in Next.js
import React from 'react';
import Link from 'next/link';

const Navigation = () => {
return (
<nav>
<Link href="/">
<a>Home</a>
</Link>
<Link href="/about">
<a>About</a>
</Link>
</nav>
);
};

export default Navigation;
```

By embracing Next.js, developers can leverage its features to build high-performance React applications with simplified server-side rendering, automatic code splitting, and an intuitive project structure. These capabilities contribute to a more efficient and enjoyable development experience.

25. Browser Developer Tools

25.1 Mastering Chrome DevTools

Chrome DevTools is a comprehensive set of tools built into the Chrome browser, designed to assist developers in inspecting, debugging, and optimizing web applications. Here are some key features:

- Elements Tab: Inspect and manipulate the DOM. View and edit HTML and CSS in real-time.
- Console Tab: Execute JavaScript, log messages, and debug code. Use console.log for basic logging.

```javascript
// Example of Console Logging
const name = 'John';
console.log('Hello, ' + name);
```

- Sources Tab: Debug JavaScript, set breakpoints, and step through code execution.
- Network Tab: Monitor network activity, analyze HTTP requests, and optimize loading times.
- Application Tab: Inspect and manipulate cookies, local storage, and other web storage.
- Performance Tab: Profile and analyze the performance of your web application. Identify bottlenecks and optimize for speed.

25.2 Debugging JavaScript in the Browser

Debugging JavaScript is crucial for identifying and fixing issues in your code. Chrome DevTools provides powerful debugging capabilities:

- Breakpoints: Set breakpoints in your code to pause execution and inspect variables.

```javascript
// Example of Breakpoint in DevTools
function calculateSum(a, b) {
    debugger; // Set breakpoint here
    return a + b;
}

const result = calculateSum(3, 4);
console.log(result);
```

- Stepping Through Code: Use "Step Over," "Step Into," and "Step Out" to navigate through your code during debugging.
- Watch Expressions: Add watch expressions to monitor the values of variables as you step through code.

25.3 Performance Profiling with DevTools

Profiling your web application's performance is crucial for optimizing user experience. The Performance Tab in DevTools helps identify bottlenecks and areas for improvement:

- Recording a Performance Profile: Start recording, interact with your application, and stop recording to view a detailed timeline of events.
- Analyzing Loading Times: Identify resource loading times, network activity, and rendering performance.
- CPU Profiling: Understand CPU usage during critical processes and optimize performance.

```javascript
// Example of CPU-Intensive Code
function timeConsumingOperation() {
    let result = 0;
    for (let i = 0; i < 1000000; i++) {
    result += Math.random();
    }
    return result;
    }


    console.time('Time taken');
    timeConsumingOperation();
    console.timeEnd('Time taken');
```

- Memory Profiling: Detect memory leaks and optimize memory usage.

By mastering Chrome DevTools, developers gain powerful insights into their code, enabling efficient debugging and performance optimization. These tools are essential for building robust and high-performing web applications.

26. Cross-Browser Compatibility

26.1 Identifying and Resolving Browser Compatibility Issues

Cross-browser compatibility is crucial for ensuring a consistent user experience across different web browsers. Identifying and resolving compatibility issues involves the following considerations:

- CSS Vendor Prefixes: Some browsers require vendor prefixes for certain CSS properties. Use tools like Autoprefixer to automatically add necessary prefixes during the build process.

```css
/* Example of CSS Vendor Prefixes */
div {
    display: -webkit-box;
    display: -ms-flexbox;
    display: flex;
}
```

- JavaScript Polyfills: Implement polyfills for missing JavaScript features in older browsers. Tools like Babel can help transpile modern JavaScript code into a compatible format.

```javascript
// Example of JavaScript Polyfill
if (!Array.prototype.includes) {
    Array.prototype.includes = function (searchElement, fromIndex) {
        // Polyfill logic
    };
}
```

26.2 Browser Testing Tools

Various tools assist in testing your web application across different browsers to catch compatibility issues early:

- BrowserStack: Allows testing on real browsers running on real devices.
- CrossBrowserTesting: Provides a cloud-based platform for interactive and automated browser testing.
- Selenium: Enables automated testing across different browsers and platforms.

26.3 Feature Detection vs. Browser Sniffing

When dealing with browser compatibility, it's essential to distinguish between feature detection and browser sniffing:

- Feature Detection: Check if a specific feature is supported before using it. This promotes a more resilient and future-proof codebase.

```javascript
// Example of Feature Detection
if ('flex' in document.body.style) {
    // Use flexbox
} else {
    // Implement an alternative
}
```

- Browser Sniffing: Avoid identifying browsers based on user-agent strings. User-agent strings can be unreliable and may lead to incorrect assumptions about a browser's capabilities.

```javascript
// Example of Browser Sniffing (Avoid)
if (navigator.userAgent.indexOf('MSIE') !== -1) {
    // Handle Internet Explorer
} else {
    // Assume other browsers
}
```

By adopting these strategies, developers can mitigate cross-browser compatibility challenges, ensuring a seamless experience for users regardless of the web browser they choose. Regular testing, feature detection, and avoiding browser sniffing contribute to a more robust and user-friendly web application.

27. Progressive Web Apps (PWAs)

27.1 What is a PWA?

A Progressive Web App (PWA) is a type of web application that leverages modern web technologies to provide a more app-like experience to users. Key characteristics of PWAs include:

- Progressive Enhancement: PWAs work for all users, regardless of the browser or device, and progressively enhance to provide advanced features for users on modern browsers.
- Responsive Design: PWAs are designed to work seamlessly on various screen sizes and devices, ensuring a consistent and engaging user experience.
- App-Like Feel: PWAs offer an app-like feel with smooth animations, navigation, and interactions, contributing to a more immersive user experience.

27.2 Building Progressive Web Apps

Building PWAs involves implementing specific technologies and practices:

- Responsive Web Design: Ensure your application layout adapts to different screen sizes and orientations.
- App Shell Model: Implement the App Shell Model to separate the application's core structure from the content, allowing for faster initial loading.
- Web App Manifest: Create a web app manifest, a JSON file that provides metadata about the application, such as its name, icon, and theme colors.

```json
// Example of Web App Manifest
{
    "name": "My PWA",
    "short_name": "PWA",
    "description": "A Progressive Web App",
    "start_url": "/",
    "display": "standalone",
    "background_color": "#ffffff",
    "theme_color": "#000000",
    "icons": [ {
    "src": "/icon.png",
    "sizes": "192x192",
    "type": "image/png"
    }]
}
```

27.3 Service Workers and Offline Support

Service workers are a key component of PWAs, enabling features like offline support and background sync:

- Service Worker Registration: Register a service worker to intercept network requests and manage the application's lifecycle.

```javascript
// Example of Service Worker Registration
if ('serviceWorker' in navigator) {
    navigator.serviceWorker.register('/service-worker.js')
    .then(registration => {
    console.log('Service Worker registered with scope:',
      registration.scope);
    })
    .catch(error => {
    console.error('Service Worker registration failed:', error);
    });
}
```

- Offline Support: Use the service worker to cache essential assets, allowing the application to work offline or in low-network conditions.

```javascript
// Example of Caching with Service Worker
self.addEventListener('install', event => {
    event.waitUntil(
    caches.open('my-cache').then(cache => {
    return cache.addAll(['/index.html', '/styles.css', '/app.js']);
    })
    );
});
```

28. Web Security Basics

28.1 HTTPS and SSL/TLS

HTTPS Overview:

HTTPS (Hypertext Transfer Protocol Secure) is an extension of HTTP that adds a layer of security using SSL/TLS (Secure Sockets Layer/Transport Layer Security) protocols. It encrypts data transmitted between the user's browser and the web server, preventing unauthorized access and data tampering.

Implementation Steps:

Obtain an SSL/TLS Certificate:

Acquire a certificate from a Certificate Authority (CA). This certificate verifies the identity of your website and enables secure communication.

Install and Configure the Certificate:

Install the SSL/TLS certificate on your web server and configure it to use HTTPS. This process varies depending on the server software (e.g., Apache, Nginx).

Code Example (Nginx):

```
# Nginx Configuration for HTTPS
server {
 listen 443 ssl;
 server_name example.com;

 ssl_certificate /path/to/your/certificate.crt;
 ssl_certificate_key /path/to/your/private.key;

 # Additional SSL settings...

 location / {
 # Your regular server configuration...
 }
}
```

28.2 Cross-Site Scripting (XSS) Prevention

XSS Overview:

Cross-Site Scripting (XSS) is a security vulnerability where attackers inject malicious scripts into web pages viewed by other users. This can lead to the theft of sensitive information or unauthorized actions on behalf of the user.

Prevention Measures:

Input Validation:

Validate and sanitize user inputs on the server side. Ensure that input data meets expected criteria and reject or sanitize any malicious input.

Output Encoding:

Encode user-generated content before rendering it in the browser. This prevents browsers from interpreting content as executable scripts.

Code Example (Node.js with Express):

```javascript
// Example of Input Validation and Output Encoding
const express = require('express');
const { xss } = require('xss');

const app = express();

app.post('/submit', (req, res) => {
  // Validate and sanitize user input
  const sanitizedInput = xss(req.body.userInput);

  // Process sanitized input...
});
```

28.3 Content Security Policy (CSP)

CSP Overview:

Content Security Policy (CSP) is a security standard that helps prevent XSS attacks by controlling which resources can be loaded and executed by a web page.

Implementation Steps:

Define a Content Security Policy:

Specify allowed sources for scripts, styles, images, and other resources using CSP headers in the web page or server configuration.

Use Nonce or Hash Values:

Utilize nonces or hash values for inline scripts and styles to specify which scripts are allowed to run.

Code Example (Meta Tag in HTML):

```html
<!-- Example of Content Security Policy Header -->
<meta http-equiv="Content-Security-Policy" content="default-src 'self';
script-src 'self' https://trusted-scripts.com; style-src 'self'
https://trusted-styles.com">
```

By incorporating HTTPS, preventing XSS through input validation and output encoding, and implementing a robust Content Security Policy, web developers can significantly enhance the security of their applications. These practices contribute to a safer online environment for users and the protection of sensitive data.

29. SEO Best Practices

29.1 Understanding Search Engine Optimization (SEO)

SEO Overview:

Search Engine Optimization (SEO) is a set of practices aimed at improving a website's visibility on search engines. The goal is to enhance organic (non-paid) traffic by optimizing various aspects of a site.

Key Concepts:

- Keywords: Identify and target relevant keywords that users might search for.
- Content Quality: Create high-quality, relevant, and engaging content that satisfies user intent.
- Backlinks: Acquire quality backlinks from reputable websites to improve authority.
- User Experience: Ensure a positive user experience with fast page loading times and mobile responsiveness.

29.2 SEO-Friendly HTML and Metadata

HTML and Metadata Optimization:

Title Tags:

Write descriptive and unique title tags for each page. Include relevant keywords.

```
<!-- Example of SEO-Friendly Title Tag -->
<head>
 <title>Best SEO Practices - Your Website</title>
</head>
```

Meta Descriptions:

Craft compelling meta descriptions that summarize the page's content and encourage clicks.

```
<!-- Example of Meta Description -->
<head>
 <meta name="description" content="Explore the best SEO practices to
improve your website's visibility on search engines. Learn key
strategies and tips for effective optimization.">
</head>
```

Heading Structure:

Use a logical heading structure (h1 to h6) to organize content. Include relevant keywords in headings.

```html
<!-- Example of Heading Structure -->
<body>
<h1>SEO Best Practices</h1>
<h2>Understanding Search Engine Optimization</h2>
<!-- More content... -->
</body>
```

29.3 Sitemaps and Robots.txt

Sitemaps:

Create an XML sitemap that lists all important pages on your website. Submit the sitemap to search engines to help them crawl and index your content efficiently.

Robots.txt:

Use a robots.txt file to instruct search engine crawlers on which parts of your site to crawl and which to ignore.

Example of Sitemap and Robots.txt:

```xml
<!-- Example of XML Sitemap -->
<urlset xmlns="http://www.sitemaps.org/schemas/sitemap/0.9">
<url>
<loc>https://www.yourwebsite.com/page1</loc>
<changefreq>weekly</changefreq>
<priority>0.8</priority>
</url>
<!-- More URLs... -->
</urlset>
```

```
plaintext
```

```
# Example of Robots.txt
User-agent: *
Disallow: /private/
Allow: /public/
```

By understanding SEO principles, optimizing HTML and metadata, and properly configuring sitemaps and robots.txt files, you can enhance your website's visibility on search engines and attract more organic traffic. Regularly update and improve your content to stay aligned with search engine algorithms and user expectations.

30. Web Accessibility Best Practices

30.1 Designing Accessible User Interfaces

Accessible UI Design Principles:

Semantic HTML:

One fundamental aspect of web accessibility is using semantic HTML elements. These elements provide a clear structure to your content, making it more understandable for assistive technologies. For instance, using the <nav> element for navigation ensures that screen readers recognize it as a navigation landmark.

```html
<!-- Example of Semantic HTML -->
<nav>
<ul>
<li><a href="/">Home</a></li>
<li><a href="/about">About</a></li>
<!-- More navigation items... -->
</ul>
</nav>
```

Contrast and Color:

Pay attention to color contrast to ensure that text and interactive elements are easily distinguishable. Utilize tools like the Web Content Accessibility Guidelines (WCAG) contrast ratio guidelines to verify and adjust color combinations for better accessibility.

```css
/* Example of CSS for Color Contrast */
button {
    color: #ffffff;
    background-color: #3498db;/* Adjust color for sufficient contrast */
}
```

Keyboard Navigation:

Design your website to be navigable using only a keyboard. This is crucial for users who rely on keyboard navigation due to mobility impairments. Test and ensure all interactive elements are accessible through keyboard input.

```html
<!-- Example of Keyboard Accessible Button -->
<button onclick="performAction()" onkeypress="performAction()"
tabindex="0">Click me</button>
```

30.2 ARIA Roles and Attributes

ARIA for Accessible Components:

Role Attribute:

The Accessible Rich Internet Applications (ARIA) specification provides roles to describe the intended purpose of an element for assistive technologies. Common roles include button, navigation, alert, etc.

```html
<!-- Example of ARIA Role Attribute -->
<div role="navigation">
 <ul>
 <li><a href="/">Home</a></li>
 <li><a href="/about">About</a></li>
 <!-- More navigation items... -->
 </ul>
</div>
```

aria-label and aria-labelledby:

Use aria-label or aria-labelledby to provide labels to elements, ensuring that screen readers convey accurate information. This is particularly important for elements like buttons and dynamic content.

```html
<!-- Example of ARIA Labels -->
<button aria-label="Close">X</button>


<!-- Example of ARIA-labelledby -->
<h2 id="section-title">Section Title</h2>
<div aria-labelledby="section-title">Content of the section</div>
```

30.3 Testing Web Accessibility

Accessibility Testing Practices:

WAVE Browser Extension:

> The WAVE browser extension is a valuable tool for identifying and fixing accessibility issues on your web pages. It provides in-depth analysis and suggestions for improvements.

Screen Reader Testing:

> Test your website using screen reader software such as NVDA (NonVisual Desktop Access) or VoiceOver to ensure a positive experience for users with visual impairments. This hands-on approach helps you understand how your content is perceived audibly.

Automated Accessibility Testing:

> Integrate automated tools like Axe, Pa11y, or Lighthouse into your development workflow. These tools can catch common accessibility issues during development and provide actionable insights.

```
# Example of Lighthouse CLI for Accessibility Testing
lighthouse https://www.yourwebsite.com --config-path=./lighthouse-
config.js --only=accessibility
```

By embracing accessible UI design principles, leveraging ARIA roles and attributes appropriately, and regularly testing web accessibility using various tools, you can create a more inclusive and user-friendly web experience for all users, regardless of their abilities or disabilities. Accessibility should be an integral part of the design and development process to ensure a web that is open and accessible to everyone.

31. Introduction to GraphQL

31.1 Basics of GraphQL

Understanding GraphQL:

GraphQL is a revolutionary query language for APIs that was developed by Facebook. It provides a flexible and efficient alternative to traditional REST APIs. The key components of GraphQL include:

- Schema Definition Language (SDL): GraphQL uses SDL to define the structure of the API. This involves specifying types, their relationships, and the operations that can be performed.

```
type Query {
    getUser(id: ID!): User
}

type Mutation {
    updateUser(id: ID!, input: UserInput): User
}

type User {
  id: ID!
  username: String!
  email: String!
}

input UserInput {
  username: String
  email: String
}
```

In the example above, we have a basic schema with a Query type for reading data and a Mutation type for modifying data. The User type represents a user object, and UserInput is used for updating user data.

31.2 Querying Data with GraphQL

Executing GraphQL Queries:

One of the main advantages of GraphQL is that clients can request only the data they need, avoiding over-fetching. GraphQL queries are hierarchical and closely resemble the shape of the response data.

Example GraphQL Query:

```
query {
    getUser(id: "123") {
        username
        email
    }
}
```

In this query, the client is asking for the username and email of the user with the ID "123." The server responds with precisely the requested data structure.

31.3 Integrating GraphQL with JavaScript

JavaScript and GraphQL:

To interact with a GraphQL API using JavaScript, you can use libraries like Apollo Client or Relay. These libraries simplify the process of making HTTP requests to the GraphQL endpoint and handling the responses.

Example Using Apollo Client:

```
import { ApolloClient, InMemoryCache, gql } from '@apollo/client';

const client = new ApolloClient({
  uri: 'https://example.com/graphql',
  cache: new InMemoryCache(),
});

client
  .query({
  query: gql`
  query {getUser(id: "123") {
  username
  email
  }} `,})
  .then((result) => console.log(result.data));
```

Here, Apollo Client is used to send a query to a GraphQL endpoint. The response is then logged to the console. Apollo Client also provides features like caching, state management, and real-time updates, enhancing the overall development experience. By embracing the basics of GraphQL, understanding how to craft efficient queries, and integrating GraphQL seamlessly with JavaScript through dedicated libraries, developers can build robust and flexible APIs that cater to the specific needs of their applications. The power of GraphQL lies in its ability to provide a tailored and efficient data-fetching mechanism for modern web development.

32. WebSockets and Real-Time Communication

32.1 Understanding WebSockets

WebSockets Overview:

WebSockets provide a full-duplex communication channel over a single, long-lived connection, enabling real-time bidirectional data transfer between a client and a server. Unlike traditional HTTP requests, WebSockets allow for efficient, low-latency communication.

WebSocket Lifecycle:

Connection Establishment:

- A WebSocket connection is initiated through a handshake between the client and server.
- Once established, the connection remains open, facilitating constant communication.

Bi-Directional Communication:

- Both the client and server can send messages independently.
- Real-time updates can be pushed from the server to the client without the need for continuous polling.

Connection Termination:

- The WebSocket connection can be closed by either the client or server, or it may close due to network issues.

32.2 Building a Real-Time Chat Application

Real-Time Chat with WebSockets:

Building a real-time chat application is a common use case for WebSockets. The application involves the following key components:

- WebSocket Server:
  - Implemented to handle WebSocket connections.
  - Manages user connections and relays messages between clients.
- WebSocket Client:
  - Connects to the WebSocket server.
  - Sends and receives messages in real-time.
- Messaging Protocol:
  - Defines the structure of messages exchanged between clients and the server.

WebSocket Server (Node.js with ws library):

```javascript
const WebSocket = require('ws');
const server = new WebSocket.Server({ port: 3000 });

server.on('connection', (socket) => {
 socket.on('message', (message) => {
   // Broadcast the message to all connected clients
   server.clients.forEach((client) => {
   if (client !== socket && client.readyState === WebSocket.OPEN) {
   client.send(message);
   }
   });
 });
});
```

Example WebSocket Client (JavaScript in the Browser):

```javascript
const socket = new WebSocket('ws://localhost:3000');

socket.addEventListener('open', (event) => {
 console.log('WebSocket connection opened');
});

socket.addEventListener('message', (event) => {
 console.log('Received message:', event.data);
});

// Send a message to the server
socket.send('Hello, WebSocket!');
```

32.3 Scaling Real-Time Applications

Scaling Challenges:

As real-time applications grow, scaling becomes a crucial consideration. Several strategies can be employed to scale real-time applications:

- Load Balancing:
  - Distribute WebSocket connections across multiple servers using a load balancer.
- Horizontal Scaling:
  - Increase the number of WebSocket servers to handle a larger number of concurrent connections.
- State Management:
  - Use a centralized state store (e.g., Redis) to synchronize state across multiple server instances.
- Optimizing Message Handling:
  - Optimize message processing to handle a high volume of real-time updates efficiently.

By comprehending the fundamentals of WebSockets, building a real-time chat application, and addressing scaling challenges, developers can create responsive and scalable real-time communication systems that cater to the demands of modern applications. WebSockets play a crucial role in enhancing user experience by enabling instantaneous updates and interactions in web applications.

33. Server-Side Rendering (SSR)

33.1 What is SSR?

Understanding Server-Side Rendering (SSR):

Server-Side Rendering is a technique where the server generates the full HTML for a page on every request and sends it to the client. This is in contrast to client-side rendering, where the browser is responsible for rendering the page using JavaScript.

Key Concepts:

- Initial Page Load:
    - HTML content is generated on the server and sent to the client.
    - Improves page load performance and search engine optimization (SEO).
- Enhanced User Experience:
    - Faster perceived page load time as content is visible sooner.

33.2 Implementing SSR with Node.js and Express

Node.js and Express for SSR:

Node.js, along with the Express framework, is commonly used to implement Server-Side Rendering.

Example SSR Implementation with Express:

```
const express = require('express');
const app = express();
app.set('view engine', 'ejs');

app.get('/', (req, res) => {
// Render the 'index' view on the server
 res.render('index', { data: 'Hello from Server!' });
});

app.listen(3000, () => {
 console.log('Server listening on port 3000');
});
```

Example 'index.ejs' View Template:

```
<!DOCTYPE html>
<html lang="en">
<head>
 <meta charset="UTF-8">
 <meta name="viewport" content="width=device-width, initial-scale=1.0">
 <title>Server-Side Rendering Example</title>
</head>
<body>
 <h1><%= data %></h1>
</body>
</html>
```

33.3 Benefits and Drawbacks of SSR

Benefits of SSR:
- Improved SEO:
  - Search engines can easily crawl and index content.
- Faster Initial Page Load:
  - Users see content sooner as HTML is generated on the server.

Drawbacks of SSR:
- Increased Server Load:
  - Generating HTML on every request can strain server resources.
- Complexity in State Management:
  - Managing client-side state requires additional considerations.

34. Microservices Architecture

34.1 Introduction to Microservices

Understanding Microservices:

Microservices architecture involves breaking down a monolithic application into smaller, independent services. Each service is responsible for a specific business capability and communicates with others through well-defined APIs.

Key Characteristics:

- Independence:
    - Microservices operate independently and can be developed, deployed, and scaled independently.
- Scalability:
    - Individual services can be scaled based on demand.

34.2 Designing Microservices

Design Principles:

- Single Responsibility:
    - Each microservice should have a single responsibility or business capability.
- Decentralized Data Management:
    - Services should manage their own data and communicate through APIs.

34.3 Implementing Microservices with Node.js and Docker

Implementing microservices with Node.js and Docker involves creating a distributed system of small, independent services that communicate with each other. This allows for better scalability, maintainability, and flexibility in building complex applications. Here's an in-depth explanation of the steps involved in implementing microservices with Node.js and Docker:

Understanding Microservices Architecture:

Microservices are small, independently deployable services that work together to form a complete application. Each microservice typically handles a specific business capability and communicates with other microservices through well-defined APIs. This architecture allows for independent development, deployment, and scaling of services.

Choosing Node.js for Microservices:

Node.js is a popular runtime for building scalable and efficient server-side applications. Its non-blocking I/O and event-driven architecture make it well-suited for handling a large number of concurrent requests, which is crucial in microservices architectures.

Setting Up a Node.js Microservice:

Start by creating a basic Node.js microservice. Use a framework like Express.js to simplify the creation of RESTful APIs. Each microservice should be responsible for a specific functionality.
Example of a simple Node.js microservice using Express:

```
// microservice.js
const express = require('express');
const app = express();
const port = 3000;

app.get('/', (req, res) => {
 res.send('Hello from Microservice!');
});

app.listen(port, () => {
 console.log(`Microservice listening at http://localhost:${port}`);
});
```

Containerizing with Docker:

Docker simplifies the deployment of microservices by containerizing each service along with its dependencies. This ensures consistency across different environments.
Create a Dockerfile for your Node.js microservice:
Dockerfile

```
# Dockerfile
FROM node:14

WORKDIR /app

COPY package*.json ./

RUN npm install

COPY . .

EXPOSE 3000

CMD ["node", "microservice.js"]

Build the Docker image:
bash
Copy code
docker build -t your-microservice .

Run the Docker container:
bash
Copy code
docker run -p 3000:3000 -d your-microservice
```

Communication Between Microservices:

Microservices communicate with each other through APIs. Consider using HTTP/REST or message queues like RabbitMQ or Kafka for asynchronous communication. Tools like Axios or the native fetch API in Node.js can be used for HTTP requests.

Orchestrating Microservices:

To manage and orchestrate multiple microservices, consider using orchestration tools like Kubernetes or Docker Compose. These tools help with scaling, load balancing, and service discovery.

Securing Microservices:

Implement security measures such as authentication and authorization to protect microservices. Use tools like JWT (JSON Web Tokens) for authentication and OAuth 2.0 for authorization.

Monitoring and Logging:

Implement logging and monitoring to gain insights into the performance and health of your microservices. Tools like Prometheus, Grafana, and ELK stack (Elasticsearch, Logstash, Kibana) can be useful.

Continuous Integration/Continuous Deployment (CI/CD):

Set up CI/CD pipelines to automate the testing, building, and deployment of microservices. Popular CI/CD tools include Jenkins, GitLab CI, and GitHub Actions.

Testing Microservices:

Implement testing strategies, including unit testing, integration testing, and end-to-end testing, to ensure the reliability and correctness of your microservices.

Conclusion:

Implementing microservices with Node.js and Docker involves careful consideration of architecture, communication, containerization, orchestration, security, monitoring, and more. By breaking down applications into smaller, manageable services, teams can iterate faster, scale more efficiently, and maintain a high level of agility in response to changing requirements. Always refer to best practices and consider the specific needs of your project when implementing microservices.

Congratulations, intrepid learner, on completing this odyssey through

"HTMLicious CSSentials & JavaScriptopia: Mastering the Web Development Symphony." You've not just turned the pages of a book; you've opened a door to a world of limitless possibilities in web development.

As you reach this conclusion, envision it not as an end but as a prelude to your own web development saga. Your journey doesn't conclude here; it evolves. The chapters you've explored are waypoints guiding you to the next level of mastery.

Consider this handbook as a compass and the Mozilla Developer Network (MDN) as your map. Now armed with the basics of HTML, CSS, and JavaScript, the landscape of web development is yours to explore further.

Here are a few parting notes and advice:
Deepen Your Understanding:
- Dive into advanced topics and concepts. Explore the depths of HTML, CSS, and JavaScript by tackling more complex projects. Consider exploring frameworks and libraries like React, delving into responsive design, or experimenting with modern JavaScript features.
-

Practice, Practice, Practice:
- The crucible of practice is where true mastery emerges. Apply what you've learned by working on real-world projects. Whether it's building a personal website, creating a portfolio, or developing dynamic web applications, the more you practice, the more confident and skilled you'll become.
-

Continuous Learning:
- Web development is a dynamic field that constantly evolves. Stay updated on new technologies, best practices, and industry trends. Follow blogs, participate in online communities, and attend web development events to stay connected with the latest advancements.
-

Explore Specializations:
- Web development is vast, and there are various specializations within the field. Explore areas like front-end development, back-end development, UX/UI design, and more. Discover what aspects of web development resonate with you and align with your career goals.

Build a Portfolio:
- Create a portfolio showcasing your projects and skills. A well-crafted portfolio is not only a testament to your abilities but also a valuable tool when seeking opportunities in the web development industry.

Remember, this isn't just an endnote; it's an invitation to a new chapter. Embrace the ever-changing landscape of web development, seek new challenges, and let curiosity be your guide. Your journey has just begun—happy and adventurous exploring!

Best wishes,
RAFA
The Author

Printed in Great Britain
by Amazon

36858864R00088